Southdown Memories

Glyn Kraemer-Johnson and John Bishop

Front cover: A type that has become synonymous with Southdown is the Northern Counties-bodied Leyland PD3, the company electing to stick with the front-engined Titan in preference the Lancashire manufacturer's rear-engined Atlantean model. One of the first batch, 826 (TCD 826), is seen on the forecourt of Fareham bus station when new in the summer of 1958. The story goes that it was crews in the Portsmouth area that first applied to these vehicles the nickname 'Queen Mary', on account of their size, although this is disputed. *Bruce Jenkins*

Back cover: May 1954 saw the construction of a new bus garage-cum-station in Lewes, the county town of East Sussex. Featuring a smart waiting room and cafeteria along with facilities for staff, it was a credit to the company and the town. In this scene from January 1957 Leyland Titan TD5 No 222 (FUF 222), rebodied seven years previously by Beadle, takes on passengers for Haywards Heath. *Bruce Jenkins*

Title page: In the early 1960s Southdown, in common with a number of other operators, took delivery of convertible-open-top buses, which could be used all year round rather than merely during the summer months, as had been the case with the Guy Arabs. Like all double-deck deliveries of the period the new buses were Northern Counties-bodied Leyland Titan PD3s; this 1960s view features 406 (406 DCD) passing the Southdown depot in Royal Parade, Eastbourne, while on circular route 197, which would give passengers a memorable trip along the coast and through the South Downs. *Bruce Jenkins*

CONTENTS

Narrative by Glyn Kraemer-Johnson
Photographs selected and captioned by John Bishop

First published 2009

ISBN (13) 978 0 7110 3255 2

Published by Ian Allan Publishing an imprint of Ian Allan Publishing Ltd, Hersham, Surrey KT12 4RG

Printed in England by Ian Allan Printing Ltd, Hersham, Surrey KT12 4RG

0904/B

Visit the Ian Allan Publishing website at www.ianallanpublishing.com

Left: Although not of the best quality, this shot evokes many memories for the photographer, being among the first of many that would be taken of Southdown vehicles over the ensuing half-century. Beadle-bodied Leyland Titan TD5 No 216 (FCD 516) is on a short-working of route 22, which at the time normally penetrated as far west as Petersfield, while all-Leyland PD2/12 No 747 (MCD 747) has blinds set for the 23 to Crawley. *John Bishop*

INTRODUCTION

To describe it as the Rolls-Royce of bus companies might be stretching a point, but Southdown Motor Services Ltd was certainly a cut above most of its fellow operators. And it had started with the intention of being just that.

Take the livery. This had been adopted by the company upon its formation in 1915 but was a modified version of that used by Worthing Motor Services, one of Southdown's constituent companies. Whatever its origin, its use was a stroke of sheer genius. There were any number of companies that painted their buses green, but the dark, drab shades used by such as Maidstone & District and London General Country Services were not for Southdown; its was a bright apple green that blended so well with the backdrop of the rolling South Downs through which its buses passed. Roofs and window surrounds were 'primrose' (in reality a rich cream), whilst on service buses a darker shade of green was applied to the radiators, mudguards and wheels, the whole being set off – in prewar days, at least — by gold lining.

Many of the larger companies painted their coaches in a reversed version of their bus livery, resulting in most being predominantly cream. Again, it was not Southdown's style to follow the herd, and its coaches were painted apple green below the waist and dark green above, the two shades being separated by a cream band. With the advent of the underfloor-engined coach a simpler scheme of all-over apple green was adopted. There were other companies that eschewed the reversed livery option, notably Aldershot & District, East Kent and Wilts & Dorset, of which the last, having been associated with Southdown in its early days, adopted a layout similar to that of the Brighton company but using two-tone red instead of green. Even when all-over green was applied there was still no mistaking a Southdown coach. In some cases bodybuilders adapted their standard designs to meet Southdown's requirements, and, at least until the early 1960s, Southdown's coaches all had the company's standard mouldings and beading that immediately set them apart from the manufacturers' standard products.

Fleetnames too were something special. Most operators opted for a fairly simple style, usually featuring large first and last letters, the intermediate characters being underlined. Not so Southdown. It chose a style, which again owed its origins to Worthing Motor Services, with ornate block letters, the 'S' being slightly taller than the rest, and all having a black shadow to the left and below. This was all right for buses, but the coach fleet deserved something more stylish, and Douglas Mackenzie, one of the company's founders, came up with his famous 'Mackenzie script' fleetname, which would applied to all coaches (and some buses) until the advent of the National Bus Company. A few other operators (though not many) adopted different fleetname styles for their coaches, but none had the flair and elegance of the Southdown example.

Left: The history of Southdown Motor Services goes back to 1915 and the merger of three smaller operators, including Worthing Motor Services, which concern's livery was adopted by the new company. Dating ostensibly from 1914 (but in fact based on a chassis somewhat older than the original), Newman-bodied Tilling-Stevens Petrol-Electric IB 552 has been restored by the energetic team at Amberley Working Museum, in West Sussex, where it was photographed in June 1993. *John Bishop / Online Transport*

Above: The Southdown 'sparkle' was in evidence not only in the company's home territory of Sussex and east Hampshire but also on coaches the length and breadth of the country. Looking immaculate while on a tour (or 'coach cruise', in Southdown parlance) of Devon and Cornwall in 1939 is Burlingham-bodied Leyland Tigress No 318 (CUF 318), dating from 1936.
S. L. Poole / The Omnibus

Whilst these two features alone set Southdown apart from its fellows, the impression would have been short-lived had the vehicles been allowed to become shabby or neglected. They never were. Both buses and coaches were immaculately maintained and presented, such that the phrase 'the Southdown sparkle' was coined to describe their appearance. However, the company's prowess was by no means confined to the external appearance of its vehicles. With the postwar travel boom Southdown became a leader in the field of coach holidays, and its luxuriously appointed touring coaches, specially selected drivers and faultless organisation set standards of comfort and service that many of today's operators would do well to emulate.

From the earliest days most vehicles acquired new were allocated matching fleet and registration numbers. Even during World War 2, when most operators were registering their vehicles with haphazard and non-sequential numbers, Southdown managed to ensure that all but seven of its 100 utility Guy Arabs were given registration numbers that to some extent matched their fleet numbers. Southdown staff, incidentally, never referred to the company's vehicles or its buses or coaches; they were always known as 'cars', a term that continued in use well into the NBC era.

Unlike many of its fellow operators Southdown was not a particularly innovative company. It introduced its ill-fated Leyland PD2/12 double-deck coach in 1950 and operated a Guy and a couple of PD3s with experimental (and not very successful) heating and ventilation systems. It did contribute to the introduction of the first hovercraft service between Southsea and the Isle of Wight, having the prestige of seeing the Southdown fleetname carried by the craft for a couple of weeks. In the main, however, the company was more concerned with developing the service and reputation for which it had become famous. It was particularly renowned for its timetabling and connecting services, especially what became known as the 'Heathfield Pool, whereby a number of services operated jointly with Maidstone & District and linking Brighton, Eastbourne, Tunbridge Wells, Hawkhurst and Hastings inter-worked at Heathfield, offering the passenger a much better (and more economic) service than would have been the case had they been operated independently.

Southdown Memories is the fifth book that John and I have written about the company, but let me not give the impression that it is just another publication dealing solely with its vehicles and services. This is a collection of memories in words and pictures, both our own and those of others who have kindly contributed their own anecdotes and memories. They are memories going back more than 60 years, and if, in the course of that time, they have become a little blurred, resulting in some minor inaccuracies, we apologise. Similarly, if there is a bias towards the Brighton area it is because that is where we both grew up and which was the source of many of those memories of what to us was indeed the Rolls-Royce of bus companies.

Glyn Kraemer-Johnson
Hailsham, East Sussex
January 2009

ACKNOWLEDGEMENTS

We should like to express our thanks to all those who have contributed photographs for reproduction, particularly Bruce Jenkins and Roger Knight. Thanks also go to Ben Cowdrey, Mick Isaacs, Robin Tidey and all those who, intentionally or otherwise, have provided anecdotes for inclusion in this book.

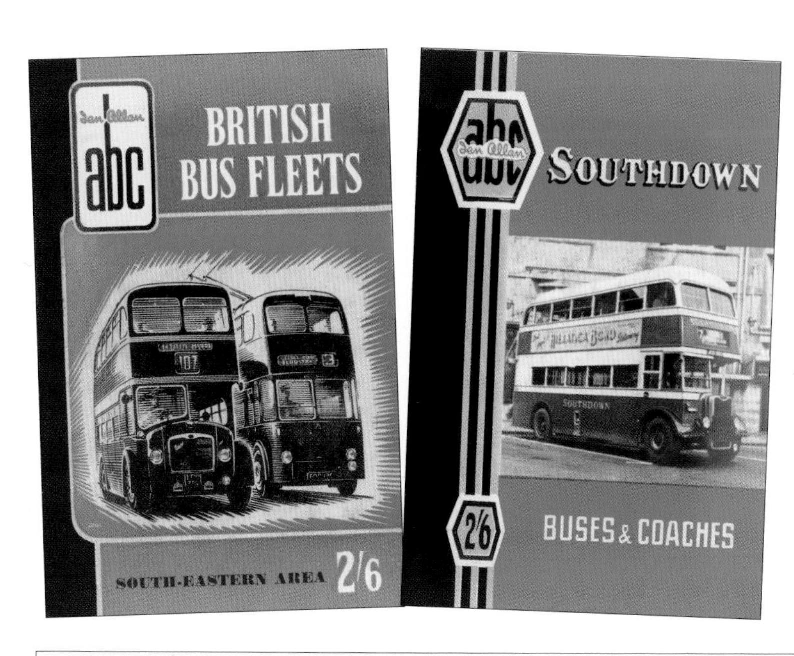

Far left: Essential to most enthusiasts were the Ian Allan 'abc' books, including one devoted entirely to Southdown. Where would we have been without such lists detailing the types and numbers of the vast fleet of buses and coaches operated by the company in the late 1950s and early '60s? And, yes, your author's copy has the numbers underlined! *John Bishop collection*

Left: A name revered by Southdown enthusiasts is that of Eric Surfleet, who as well as being a superb photographer had a shop in South Street, Lancing. Clearly he had other talents too, for a chance visit by one of the authors to a friend in the West Country elicited this rendition of one of Southdown's Duple-bodied Leyland Royal Tiger coaches, in the style of a tour brochure from the 1950s. *John Bishop collection*

Left: The service vehicles used by Southdown could fill a chapter of their own, but space considerations dictate otherwise! Used as an enquiry office at Cosham, where it was photographed on 23 February 1949, was this ex-Hastings Guy BTX single-deck trolleybus, no doubt made redundant in its native town by the postwar influx of double-deck Sunbeams.
J. Cull / The Omnibus Society

1. 'FROM LITTLE ACORNS...'

Southdown Motor Services Ltd was a war baby, first seeing the light of day on 2 June 1915. It was formed from three main constituents – Worthing Motor Services, the London & South Coast Haulage Co and the country services of the Brighton, Hove & Preston United Omnibus Co Ltd.

It was hardly the ideal time for the formation of a new company. The Army had requisitioned the best horses and had then turned its attention to motor chassis that could be fitted with bodies suitable for military purposes, leaving all three companies with a surfeit of bodies for which no chassis were available, so it was hardly surprising that the new company inherited a motley collection of vehicles, mainly of Daimler and Milnes-Daimler manufacture. Most were single-deckers or coaches, the latter including a number of charabancs. The term 'charabanc', frequently abbreviated to 'chara', later came to be used to describe a coach of any kind, and especially those used for day excursions. However, the original charabanc was distinguished by having separate doors to each row of seats, much like a railway carriage.

The double-deckers, of which there were half a dozen, were naturally all of the open-top, open-staircase style. However, the open-top and open-sided vehicles were apparently very popular with the young ladies of the time, allowing them to wave their handkerchiefs at soldiers as they passed!

The motor bus was still very much in its infancy, and experiments were still being made with other forms of propulsion. The last horse buses had disappeared from the streets of Brighton as recently as 1913 and were still operating in Worthing. In 1904 the Sussex Motor Road Car Co had inaugurated a service between Worthing and Pulborough via Findon, Washington and Storrington, later to have the honour of becoming Southdown's service 1. Initially it was operated by Clarkson Steam Buses, which provided additional excitement for their passengers who were never sure whether the buses would complete the journey! Many of the breakdowns were caused by the hard water of the area, which proved injurious to the boilers of the steamers. The company tried to overcome the problem by installing large underground tanks beneath the White Horse Inn at Storrington in the hope that sufficient rain water could be collected to fuel the buses. Unfortunately it was a year of drought, and after six months the steam buses were replaced by a Milnes-Daimler single-decker. This service proved very popular with the locals, providing many with their first experience of the horseless carriage.

Along the coast at Brighton the Brighton, Hove & Preston company had tried out three battery-electric 'Electrobuses', and these were followed by some Tilling-Stevens petrol-electrics in which a petrol engine powered a generator producing electricity, this then being used to power the rear wheels. The petrol-electric was much simpler to drive than the normal motor bus and was therefore well suited to being driven by former horse-bus drivers. This type of vehicle was to be successful in Brighton, being perpetuated by the successor to BHPU, Thomas Tilling Ltd, with which it would be the standard type, both in Brighton and in London, until the arrival in 1930 of the first AEC Regents.

Brighton and Portsmouth corporations were both firmly wedded to the electric tram, but from its formation Southdown remained faithful to the motor bus. The newly formed company set about buying new vehicles, trying to avoid the types that might appeal to the military! Apart from the requisitioning of vehicles there were fewer restrictions due to the war than would be the case in the one that was to follow in 1939 and a full programme of charabanc excursions was operated from Brighton, Worthing and Bognor. However, with the introduction of more stringent petrol rationing the horse-drawn carriages inherited by the company came into their own for this kind of work and proved most popular on trips to such beauty spots as Devil's Dyke, north-west of Brighton.

Some vehicles were converted to run on ordinary household gas, which involved fitting a huge balloon-like container to the roof of the bus. Peculiar looking to start with, they looked positively weird as they emptied and began to droop over the sides of the bus, taking on an appearance not unlike that of a cottage loaf that had been made with insufficient yeast! At that time, of course, gas was much more widely used than today, particularly for lighting where it was replacing oil and candles. Its domestic and industrial uses obviously had priority and towards the end of the war restrictions were imposed on its use in motor vehicles equal to those applied to fuel oil. Southdown therefore abandoned its use and reverted to the less cumbersome petrol.

The end of the conflict found the bus industry in a pretty sorry state. As we have already heard, large numbers of vehicles, either complete or in chassis form, had been commandeered by the Government, many never to return. Those that remained had suffered badly from lack of maintenance, the petrol shortage and the condition of the roads, the

Left: A commercial postcard depicting King's Road, Brighton, just east of the junction with West Street, in the early 1920s. Representing an early purchase by the fledgling Southdown Motor Services, in 1919, the charabanc immediately to the left of the lamp standard, Harrington-bodied Leyland N No 106 (CD 3536), was one of a total of 30 such chassis received in the period immediately following World War 1.
John Bishop collection

latter also due to poor maintenance. It was said that there were potholes eight inches across in the Kingsway, Hove, which, as can be imagined, played havoc with the wooden wheels and primitive suspension of the early motor buses. As a result many were no longer fit for service.

On the other hand the Government was left with huge numbers of buses and lorries it no longer required. This was not particularly good news for Southdown. Thousands of servicemen were returning home with money in their pockets and many saw the opportunity to make some more by buying an ex-WD lorry, fitting it with a bus body and starting their own services.

Southdown had been fortunate to obtain a handful of new vehicles during the war. The first of these were bought in chassis form and were fitted with the spare bodies taken from commandeered chassis. During these early years body swapping was rife and it must have been a fascinating time for bus enthusiasts, if indeed there were any, with single-deckers being rebodied as double-deckers and lorries becoming coaches!

Postwar recovery began in earnest in 1919 with more than 40 new buses entering the fleet. They included vehicles of Daimler and Tilling-Stevens manufacture, together with the company's first Leylands, a make that was to remain at the forefront of the Southdown fleet throughout the company's existence.

Between the two world wars additions to the fleet were made up of a mixture of new and secondhand vehicles, most of the latter coming to the company with the fleets of acquired operators. The first of these acquisitions was made as early as May 1915, before Southdown was

Above: Post-marked 1931, this postcard of the Promenade at Bognor Regis features No 54 (UF 2199), a Short-bodied Tilling-Stevens Petrol-Electric dating from 1927, working route 10A to Worthing via Arundel. The chassis of this vehicle and similar No 200 (UF 2200) were unusual in being constructed by Southdown using Tilling-Stevens running units.
John Bishop collection

formally established, when the business of A. Davies of Bognor Regis was taken over. This gave Southdown a foothold in the West Sussex resort as well as a route from there to Portsmouth, which was later linked to Worthing and Brighton to form the famous service 31.

The takeover of smaller operators formed the basis of the company's expansion over the next 20 years. Many were small one-man or family concerns with maybe half a dozen vehicles whilst there were others, such as Chapman's of Eastbourne, the acquisition of which brought more than 40 coaches into the fleet. However, it was not the vehicles but the stage services, tours and excursion licences that were the real prize.

By the outbreak of World War 2 Southdown's operating area had reached the boundaries that would remain until privatisation in 1986. It extended from Fareham in the west to Hastings in the east as well as inland to Petersfield, Horsham, Crawley, East Grinstead and Tunbridge Wells. There were very few towns and villages within that area that weren't served by the familiar green and cream buses. These towns and villages had themselves grown during this period, especially following the electrification of the Southern Railway's main lines between London and the Sussex Coast making it easier for people to work in London whilst living in the clean air and beautiful surroundings of the Sussex countryside. This resulted in ribbon development along the coastal strip and the building of estates on the outskirts of the larger towns. All generated extra traffic for Southdown.

World War 2 brought a temporary halt to this expansion, but in the early 1950s it recommenced with a vengeance, large estates, both private and council being built in most of the larger conurbations. In the late 1940s work began on the huge development at Leigh Park north of Havant, built as an overspill suburb for the city of Portsmouth. At around the same time the small market town of Crawley was designated a New Town to provide housing and employment for overcrowded Londoners who were still suffering from the effects of the Blitz. The New Town stretched from Three Bridges in the east, a major junction on the main London–Brighton railway line, to the agricultural town of Ifield in the west. Crawley itself was centred on the George Inn, which since the 17th century had been a staging-post on the London–Brighton stage-coach service. Indeed the town was still the location for Southdown's refreshment stop on its London express services.

Both of these developments had spawned new services, those in Leigh Park being operated jointly with the City of Portsmouth Passenger Transport Department under the Portsmouth Joint Services Agreement, introduced in 1946, under which mileage and receipts within the Portsmouth area were pooled. Services in the Crawley area were later subject to some reallocation between Southdown and London Transport. In 1961 an arrangement similar to that in Portsmouth was introduced in Brighton, where hitherto Southdown had charged higher fares to protect the local operations of Brighton, Hove & District. Under the agreement services of all three operators were rationalised and co-ordinated.

After World War 2 there were few small stage carriage operators left within the Southdown area. The bus services of Beacon Motor Services of Crowborough were acquired in 1949, followed by those of S[illegible] of East Grinstead in 1951. By this time there were probably [illegible] independent stage carriage operators in Sussex than in almost any other part of the country outside London.

Although Southdown's territory had remained much as it was in 1939, a number of services were operated jointly with fellow BET subsidiary Maidstone & District, taking apple green and cream as far afield as Gravesend, Hawkhurst and Battle.

Left: This attractive scene was recorded at Barnham, near Chichester, and features, besides a fine windmill, Southdown No 696 (UF 6596), a 31-seat Short-bodied Tilling-Stevens B10A2 dating from 1930. In the distance is a Model Y Ford, while in the foreground two small boys play without a care in the world. *John Bishop collection*

Left: The Thornycroft chassis was not favoured by Southdown engineering staff, but a number were acquired upon the takeover of smaller operators. No 547 (RV 1844), a CD model with Wadham coachwork, came with the fleet of Denmead Queen, Hambledon, in March 1935 and is seen at Clarence Pier, Southsea, in August of that year. Along with two similar vehicles it would pass to Wilts & Dorset in 1939 for troop transport. *J. Cull / The Omnibus Society*

2. TOOLS OF THE TRADE

A workman is only as good as his tools, and it could be said that a bus company is only as good as its vehicles. Certainly this appeared to be Southdown's philosophy from its inception.

The period between the wars must have seen more advances in the development of the motor bus than any other comparable period. At the outbreak of World War 1 the horse bus was still much in evidence, and the motor buses of the time were little more than motorised horse buses with wooden wheels, solid tyres and, in the case of double-deckers, an open top and an outside staircase, upper-deck passengers being completely exposed to the elements. This led to the two decks being referred to as 'inside' and 'outside', terms that remained in use for many years after the introduction of the closed top. I well remember conductors in the 1940s and '50s calling out "Room for three inside and four on top" or "Outside only". The driver too had little protection from the weather apart from a leather apron that fastened beneath the chin.

Below: A superbly atmospheric view of a Southdown Tilling-Stevens TS3 charabanc, with crew in white summer uniform, on a party outing in Brighton *c*1920. The fleet number is not apparent, but the vehicle is believed to be No 73 (CD 4873), with Harrington body, dating from 1919. *John Bishop collection, courtesy Robin Tidey*

As explained earlier, the wooden wheels were unable to cope with the indifferent road surfaces that prevailed following the war and frequently broke or fell off completely. Reliability was greatly improved with the arrival in the years 1919-21 of no fewer than 30 new Leyland 'N' types, which, as well as having more dependable motors, were fitted with cast-iron spoked wheels. During the same period a similar number of Tilling-Stevens TS3 Petrol-Electrics were also delivered to Southdown, the company not wanting to put all its eggs into one basket.

Obviously more robust and reliable, the new buses probably did little to improve passenger comfort; this was eventually brought about by the introduction of the pneumatic tyre. The rubber tyre with an air-filled inner tube had actually been invented towards the end of the 19th century but like many inventions was slow to take off; it was not until 1919 that Goodyear and Dunlop each introduced a pneumatic tyre suitable for commercial vehicles, and not until 1926 would Southdown take delivery of its first vehicles so fitted from new, although over the next couple of years most (if not all) of the fleet would be so equipped.

The Leyland N and Tilling TS3 types of 1919-21 were fitted with full-width windscreens affording the driver much greater protection. In fact by this time single-deckers were more or less fully enclosed. Double-deckers continued to be of open-top, open-staircase configuration, this being as much a question of height as anything, as their high chassis frames would have made a covered top impractical.

In 1925 Southdown received its first 'forward-control' buses, in which the driver was positioned beside rather than behind the engine, thus enabling passenger capacity to be increased and this remained the normal layout until the introduction of the rear-engined chassis.

Probably the greatest single advance in bus design came in 1927 with the introduction by Leyland Motors of its Titan TD1 double-deck and Tiger TS1 single-deck chassis. These had a more powerful six-cylinder petrol engine of some 6 litres' capacity but, more importantly, had a much lower chassis frame which at last allowed for a covered-top double-decker. Southdown's first order was for 23 Titans with 51-seat bodywork by Brush of Loughborough which, rather surprisingly, was of the open-top open-staircase design. Delivered in 1929, these buses had particularly long lives for the time. During World War 2 canvas top covers were fitted to the upper deck, giving them a most odd

Left: In the period following World War 1 Southdown charabancs were popular for church outings and the like. This vehicle is believed to be No 1 (CD 5001), a Daimler CB inherited from Worthing Motor Services (as IB 701) and rebodied by Harrington as a charabanc in the early 1920s. It is seen outside a typical flint-walled Sussex church, although the location is uncertain, and any further information would be most welcome. *John Bishop collection*

Left: Pictured on Brighton seafront is No 133 (CD 6543), a 1921 Dodson-bodied Leyland G7, which chassis type formed the basis of Southdown's double-deck deliveries for five years. Remarkably No 135 from the same batch, albeit with a newer body, survives today in the ownership of Stagecoach Holdings. *John Bishop collection*

appearance, but after the war these were removed, and most of the batch continued in use on the company's open-top services until replaced in 1950/1 by converted utility Guys.

I have two abiding memories of the open-top TD1s. The first was of travelling on one on service 27 to Devil's Dyke and being fascinated by the sliding door that closed off the lower deck forward of the longitudinal rear seats. One of the type, 813, would later be preserved by the company and survives to this day in the care of the Amberley Working Museum in West Sussex. During the summer of 1971 it was used on a special service running between Rottingdean and the Palace Pier. Determined to ride on it, I chose a grey, chilly and windy day for my trip on the upper deck and the next day found myself in bed with a painful case of pleurisy!

As well as the revolutionary chassis Leyland also designed and built its own body for the TD1. Naturally this had an enclosed top deck, and it was offered with either outside or enclosed staircase. Besides the standard body Leyland offered a low-height version for use on routes where low bridges precluded the use of a normal-height double-decker. This design was again quite revolutionary. The low height was achieved by means of a

Above: The discomfort of riding on early, solid-tyred vehicles can scarcely be imagined, yet pneumatics were not introduced until 1926. Forward-control Tilling-bodied Tilling-Stevens TS6 No 233 (CD 9233) of 1925 is seen outside the garage and coach station at Worthing in company with normal-control TS3 No 95 (CD 8295) of 1922. *E. G. Masterman / The Omnibus Society*

Right: Driver – in smart white uniform – and passengers pose proudly for the camera in a fine-looking Harrington-bodied Tilling-Stevens B9B charabanc, No 423 (UF 2023), dating from 1927. The ornate lining and fleetname are especially noteworthy, while the fleet number can just be discerned on the front offside of the chassis. *Alan Lambert / Southdown Enthusiasts' Club*

sunken gangway on the offside of the upper deck, necessitating rows of seats for four on the nearside, and allowed the overall height to be reduced by about 12 inches, to 13ft 6in. This body, which came to be known as the 'lowbridge' and was eventually copied by almost every other bodybuilder, allowed operators to run double-deckers on services that would otherwise have been restricted to single-deckers, thereby gaining much increased passenger capacity. However, the design was not without its drawbacks. The sunken gangway protruded into the lower deck, and many a downstairs passenger rising from an offside seat cracked his/her head, despite the warning notices that were usually applied to seat backs. Meanwhile, on the upper deck, the conductor's job was made more difficult on a fully laden bus by the need to reach across three passengers to collect the fare from the one sitting by the window, and at bus stops those passengers on the nearside also had difficulty in extricating themselves, squeezing past three other passengers and making their way to the platform before the conductor rang the bell. Nevertheless, operators obviously felt that the advantages outweighed the disadvantages, and lowbridge vehicles of various makes remained in production until the advent of the Bristol Lodekka and its imitators in the 1950s.

Left: The first of a very long line of Leyland Titans for Southdown were a batch of 23 Brush-bodied TD1s delivered in 1929. New as open-toppers, they survived the war fitted with temporary canvas roofs and postwar soldiered on in original condition at a time when many newer vehicles were being rebodied. Here No 821 (UF 4821) makes for Bognor Regis on route 62 from Arundel. Similar 813, still with its original body, survives in Southdown ownership and can nowadays be found at the Amberley Working Museum. *A. D. Packer*

Left: An atmospheric view of Pool Valley in the mid-1930s, featuring a newly delivered lowbridge all-Leyland Titan TD4, No 111 (BUF 211), next to 833 (UF 5533), a lowbridge all-Leyland TD1, while third from left is a new Harrington-bodied Leyland Tiger TS7, No 1409 (BUF 989). Looking archaic by comparison are a trio of Tilling-Stevens B10A2 models — Short-bodied 679 (UF 5579) and 1200 (UF 6600) and Harrington-bodied 675 (UF 5075). The scene makes for interesting comparison with that depicted on page 31. *C. F. Klapper*

It was perhaps typical of Southdown that although, unlike most rural operators, few of its services encountered low bridges, its first covered-top double-deckers were of lowbridge layout, 'to minimise damage to roofs caused by overhanging branches'. However, the company presumably decided that the inconvenience was not worthwhile for purely cosmetic reasons and after the first 42 turned to the highbridge model, although further lowbridge buses were purchased from time to time, more than 70 TD4s and TD5s so bodied being delivered in the years 1935-9.

A further four lowbridge buses, on TD7 chassis, were ordered for delivery in 1940 but due to the outbreak of World War 2 were diverted to Cumberland Motor Services.

Although lowbridge buses were very much in the minority, Southdown still thought them important enough to distinguish them in its fleet-numbering system by placing the letter 'L' beneath the number, the fleet numbers of highbridge buses being suffixed 'H' — a system used also by City of Oxford Motor Services.

The last lowbridge double-deckers to be received by Southdown were seven utility Guy Arabs with bodywork by Strachans (three), Northern Counties and Weymann (two each). The lowbridge layout did nothing to help the appearance of the wartime austerity body, and the Strachans examples were particularly angular and unattractive.

I started school in Brighton in 1946, and not long afterwards the first school outing since the war was arranged. We were to go to 'Mr Box's field at Hassocks'. One can scarcely imagine the reaction of

Above: For its first closed-top Titans Southdown favoured the lowbridge layout. Ready to depart Uckfield bus station for Eastbourne, all-Leyland TD1 No 860 (UF 5660) of 1930, with 'piano front' body (a style recently reproduced in model form by EFE), stands alongside a later lowbridge Titan, Short-bodied TD4 No 105 (BUF 205) of 1935. Note the illuminated part of the destination screen proclaiming the company name. *J. F. Parke / The Omnibus Society*

Right: In 1932 came the company's first examples of the TD2, this being a heavier version of the TD1. Bodywork, by Short Bros, was to highbridge layout, hence the very tall appearance of No 940 (UF 8380). Note the multiplicity of slip-boards and destination screens, leaving prospective passengers in no doubt as to where the bus was heading! *The Omnibus Society*

today's schoolchildren to being promised a trip to such an exotic destination, but we were more easily pleased in those days; excitement was rife amongst my school-fellows as the appointed day approached, but their excitement was nothing compared to mine when I realised that our steed for the day would be a Southdown lowbridge utility Guy. I knew it was a Guy because it said so on the radiator, but at the age of six I didn't know it was called a 'lowbridge', only that it had a funny seating arrangement upstairs — quite handy for school transport, as six or seven children could be crammed into each row of seats! In truth I can't remember much about the bus, but from what I've come to know of utility buses since I can't imagine the ride was very comfortable.

But back to the prewar years, and the next major development was the introduction of the diesel engine. Although not as refined as its petrol counterpart, it was much more economical in operation. The first diesel-engined double-deckers for Southdown were delivered in 1936, the first coaches two years later. Most of the fleet was converted over the next few years, and soon the throaty roar of the 8.6-litre Leyland diesel could be heard throughout the company's area.

Thus it was that by the mid-1930s the bus had developed into the vehicle that, in the case of the double-decker, was to remain the standard for the next 30 years, *i.e.* fully enclosed, with front-mounted engine, half-cab layout and rear entrance. In fact it could almost be said that if one of these buses were to pull up at a stop today it would probably be the presence of the conductor rather than the bus itself that would cause eyebrows to rise.

Above: Purchased in the mid-1930s to provide extra capacity on the Eastbourne–Beachy Head service (97) were a quartet of three-axle Leyland Tiger buses, double-deckers at this time being precluded on account of the exposed nature of the route. All were bodied by Short Bros, one of the second pair, delivered in 1935, being TS7T model No 52 (BUF 552), seen at Beachy Head in later guise as No 552. *A. D. Packer*

Left: More typical of the period were the two-axle Tigers bodied by Harrington, among them TS7 coach No 1099 (BUF 899), new in 1935 and seen in Angerstein Road, Portsmouth, on 28 August 1939 — just six days before the outbreak of World War 2. *J. Cull / Omnibus Society*

Right: An ideal vehicle for Southdown's many rural services was the petrol-engined Leyland Cub, which also made for a refined small coach. This view features No 41 (DUF 41), a 20-seat Harrington-bodied coach new in 1937, by the Cathedral in West Street, Chichester, where (prior to the opening of the bus station in Eastgate Street) Southdown maintained a small enquiry office. A similar but older Cub, No 4, survives today in preservation.
J. F. Parke / The Omnibus Society

Right: Another Cub delivered in 1937, but with bus bodywork by Park Royal, was No 22 (ECD 522). This photograph was taken during World War 2, as evidenced by the white mudguards and, on the right, the 'S' sign denoting an air-raid shelter. Similar vehicle No 23 survives in preservation and at the time of writing is undergoing restoration at Amberley. *J. F. Parke / The Omnibus Society*

Left: Among the authors' all-time favourites were the Harrington bus-bodied Leyland Tigers delivered in the period 1935-9. One of the earlier examples, on TS7 chassis, was No 1423 (CCD 33), here seen in wartime grey at the Carfax, Horsham.
The Omnibus Society

Left: A nearside view of Leyland Tiger TS7 coach No 1115 (CCD 715) of 1936, recorded postwar at South Parade, Southsea, and showing to full advantage the graceful lines of the Harrington coachwork. Note that the roof has a roll-back section, as fitted to vehicles used on tours and excursions.
J. Cull / The Omnibus Society

Right: Allowing an interesting comparison with the previous photograph is this view of highbridge Short-bodied Leyland TD4c No 115 (BUF 215) at Worthing depot. The 'c' suffix to the chassis designation indicates that this is a gearless bus with torque converter, as confirmed by the words 'GEARLESS BUS' on the radiator grille. The transmission, coupled with a petrol engine, must have made this a thirsty beast, and postwar it would be fitted with conventional transmission and (in common with many other Southdown vehicles) a diesel engine. Note, again, the delicate lining on the sides and the informative destination displays.
S. L. Poole / The Omnibus Society

Right: The Leyland TD3 was a more refined model than the TD1 and TD2, with engine and gearbox set further forward in the chassis and allowing more space within the body. Southdown's first (and, as it turned out, only) examples arrived in 1934, among them No 973 (AUF 673), pictured at North End, Portsmouth, on 20 July 1947. At the time it still retained original highbridge body by Short Bros (and dark-green roof), but like all the TD3s it would soon be rebodied, in this case by Beadle.
J. Cull / The Omnibus Society

Left: By the early 1940s the Short Bros bodywork fitted to Southdown's Leyland TD2s was in need of replacement, and to prolong their lives many of these vehicles were fitted with wartime 'utility' bodywork to an angular and functional design. One of a number so treated by Willowbrook was No 953 (UF 8853), which retained its original high radiator when photographed outside Portsmouth's Hyde Park Road garage on 20 February 1949.
J. Cull / The Omnibus Society

Left: The TD3s were followed in 1935 by the first TD4s, which initiated a new number series starting at 100. Seen at Petersfield station on 30 September 1949 is 105 (BUF 205), still with original lowbridge body by Short Bros and showing the 'L' fleet-number suffix applied to lowbridge double-deckers. The crew have stopped to chat to a naval between before embarking on the two-hour journey back to Bognor Regis. *J. Cull / The Omnibus Society*

3. PRESENTING THE IMAGE

Long before the phrase 'corporate identity' was coined, Southdown was all about image. That image had existed right from the start with the creation of a fine livery with elegant fleetnames, but, however good it might be, it was worthless unless well-maintained, and in this respect too Southdown was way out in front.

Green and cream paintwork gleamed, giving rise to what became known as the 'Southdown sparkle'. Whereas the buses of some other operators would be seen with dented panels and battered roofs, this was rarely the case with Southdown. Maintenance standards were of the highest, and a bus entering the company's central works at Portslade would emerge as good as new, every part having been checked and repaired or replaced where necessary; this applied not only to the major components but also to items such as the window-winding gear, which would be greased to ensure smooth operation, and seldom could a Southdown bus be seen with a window jammed in the half-open position, as was often the case elsewhere. Similarly, if a bus were reported to have a rattle it would be driven around with a fitter on board until the cause was identified and the fault rectified.

Right: A pair of Park Royal-bodied Guy Arab IVs appear to have Pool Valley to themselves in the spring of 1956. Newly delivered 547 (PUF 647), uniquely with sliding platform door, pulls away for the coastal run on a short working, to Seaford, of route 12 whilst 523 (OUF 523) of 1954 takes a rest between journeys to and from Crawley on the 23. A number of the type would ultimately see further service in Hong Kong, but thankfully No 547 would remain in the UK to be saved for posterity. *Eric Surfleet / Glyn Kraemer-Johnson collection*

Upholstery too was immaculately maintained. True, in the 1930s, '40s and '50s vandalism wasn't the problem it is today, but, even so, torn or damaged seats just weren't seen. The interior specification was something else that raised Southdown's vehicles above those of its fellow operators. The company had developed its unique standard interior décor with seats upholstered in moquette of varying shades of brown and orange and trimmed with tan leather. Side panels were brown, whilst window frames were either half-brown / half-cream in London Transport style or dark varnished wood. The colour scheme has been described as drab and dismal, but to me it exuded quality and comfort, quiet and refined colours that were warm and welcoming, unlike the cold leatherette and clinical white used elsewhere.

And Southdown buses had heaters! I spent my formative years in the Country Area of London Transport, which not only operated buses without heaters but whose forward-entrance STLs didn't even have doors! On moving to Brighton I travelled mainly on the buses of Brighton, Hove & District and Brighton Corporation, neither of which was to fit heaters until the late 1950s. Southdown's heaters, on saloons and in the lower decks of double-deckers, were initially huge circular affairs in polished chrome fixed to the front bulkhead. On later models the heaters were incorporated into the pillar between the windows on the front bulkhead, whilst on the upper deck they were housed in a metal box beneath the front nearside seat. They would whine into life

Above: An official view featuring the upper saloon of a Park Royal body as fitted to the Guy Arab IVs and Leyland PD2/12s delivered to Southdown in 1955/6. Although the photograph is monochrome it shows well the interior décor specified by the company, notably the pattern of the upholstery. *Park Royal Vehicles / Glyn Kraemer-Johnson collection*

Left: The large Clayton Dewandre heater in the lower saloon of 114 (BUF 214), a Leyland TD4 rebodied postwar by East Lancs. *John Short*

when the bus started and would die each time it came to a halt. The heat (what there was of it) was therefore pretty intermittent, but nevertheless it *was* heat! The secret, on really cold days, was to aim for the second seat from the front so that you could rest your feet against the heater grille, and it was not until the advent of the 'Queen Mary' PD3s that a really efficient system of heating was introduced.

The early 1950s and the introduction of the first Leyland PD2/12s brought another innovation – electrically operated platform doors. The first batch arrived with open platforms, doors being fitted by Southdown staff at Portslade Works, but on all subsequent deliveries they were fitted as standard.

We all have favourite buses, and mine has always been the Bristol K. I was brought up with the type, travelling on them to school, to work and to my first dates. I loved the knocking of the Gardner engine and the vibrations it would send through the feet, but they were basic, to say the least, and on a bitterly cold winter's night the difference between a K and a Southdown PD2 was akin to that between a Ford Popular and a Bentley Continental.

Southdown's higher standards of comfort became particularly apparent in the 1950s, when it and neighbouring operators took buses of basically similar type. Both Southdown and Maidstone & District purchased Leyland PD2/12s with Leyland's own Farington bodywork,

Right: One of the second batch of all-Leyland PD2/12s, delivered in 1952, 731 (LUF 231) is pictured in George Street, Hailsham, in August 1954. In the period 1951-7 Southdown took delivery of 112 PD2s, bodied by Leyland itself, Northern Counties, Park Royal, Beadle and, finally, East Lancs. *Bruce Jenkins*

Left: Still in service in the years following World War 2 were the Harrington-bodied Leyland Lioness touring coaches new in 1930. Seating just 20 passengers, they offered exclusivity as well as comfort. Originally numbered 308, No 1808 (UF 6508) was still in pristine condition when photographed on 15 June 1948 in Bournemouth.
Alan Cross

and later in the decade, when Southdown was buying Guy Arabs and Leyland PD2s with Park Royal bodywork, both M&D and East Kent were specifying similar bodies, on AEC Regent and Guy Arab chassis respectively. These may have been similar externally, but internally it was very much a case of a five-star rating for Southdown compared with the two or three stars of the others.

Prior to the implementation in 1961 of the Brighton Area Transport Services (BATS) agreement Southdown charged higher fares to protect the local Brighton operators. As a child I (and, I am sure, many older and wiser passengers) thought that the higher charge was for the privilege of travelling on a more luxurious vehicle!

As for the coaches, these were very much in a class of their own. Such was the status attached to a Southdown coach that to have one standing outside their premises was seen by many hoteliers as something of a status symbol. Coaches were maintained to a very high standard, and any vehicle setting off on a holiday tour would be gleaming. And not only on setting off, for it would be maintained in pristine condition throughout the holiday. The company's touring coaches of the 1950s and '60s were the height of luxury, with just 26 seats in a vehicle built to accommodate around 41. Moreover these were individual reclining seats, two on one side of the gangway and one on the other, each with a freshly laundered antimacassar. Attention to detail was all-important, and on boarding the coach each holiday passenger would be handed a passenger list in the form of a seating plan showing the name of each passenger and the town from whence he/she came.

As well as its top-flight tours Southdown in the early 1950s introduced what were known as 'Beacon' tours. These were cheaper, using 37-seat Beadle-bodied Leyland Tiger Cubs, and were centred in one place with daily excursions rather than travelling from place to place each day. The coaches were less well appointed, having the normal 2+2 seating, but still had ample leg room and were extremely comfortable.

I enjoyed a couple of Beacon tours in 1956 and 1957. The first was to the Peak District on car 1012, based at Buxton. These were the days when you actually passed through towns instead of by-passing them, which was wonderful for a bus enthusiast; hence I saw Huddersfield's beautiful red-and-cream buses and trolleybuses and caught my only glimpses of Leeds trams, including 'Felthams', if I remember correctly. On another day I had even briefer glimpses of St Helens RTs and Liverpool Corporation's famous 'Green Goddess' trams before lunching amidst Southport PD2s, later returning to Chester, city of Guys, for afternoon tea.

Right: One of the initial (1955) batch of Beadle-bodied Leyland Tiger Cub coaches, 1014 (OUF 114). The coach would have been smartly turned out with the driver equally smart in full-length dust coat. The damage to the side mouldings, to which reference is made in the text, is not visible in this view, which was recorded in the Cotswolds on the way back to Brighton. *Glyn Kraemer-Johnson*

The second tour was to North Wales on car 1014. For someone who regularly takes coach holidays, looking back to those tours of fifty years ago is fascinating. There were, of course, no motorways, and the journey to Dolgelly (or Dolgellau, to our Welsh readers) took two days, an overnight stop being made at Brockhampton on the outward journey and at Cheltenham (with its dark-red Albions and AECs) on the way back. When running excursions from Dolgelly our coach displayed labels proclaiming it to be 'On hire to Crosville Motor Services', and on a trip to Llandudno I witnessed the amazing sight (to me, at any rate) of that company's Bristol L single-deckers with post boxes attached to the back! Also in Llandudno were friends from home in the form of ex-Southdown utility Guys, which had replaced the Llandudno and Colwyn Bay trams. But the abiding memory is of descending the tortuous Horseshoe Pass. A lorry carrying telegraph poles had run off the road, leaving a gap of what must have been 7ft 11in between it and the stone wall on the other side of the road. Unable to reverse, our driver waited patiently for what must have been 20 minutes or so, during which time nothing was apparently being done to recover the lorry. Drastic action was called for, and the driver edged the coach slowly through the gap. I can still hear the scream of tearing metal as the decorative beading was ripped from the side of the Tiger Cub, and the driver must have spent the rest of the tour in trepidation of the likely repercussions upon our return to Brighton.

If a coach failed while on tour in another part of the country and could not be repaired on site it would frequently be towed back to Sussex under cover of darkness; it would not do for the general public to know that Southdown coaches broke down! They did break down, of course, and one Leyland Leopard/Harrington Cavalier that failed on a West Country tour was replaced by a Southern National dual-purpose Bristol SUL4A. Wonder if the passengers noticed!

It wasn't only touring coaches that maintained a high standard. During the summer months every morning would see a line of Southdown coaches on the seafronts at Worthing, Brighton and Eastbourne, green paint shining and brightwork gleaming, as they waited to depart on day and half-day excursions. Each would have a painted or chalked board giving details of the tour, which would be propped against the wheel – never the paintwork. The drivers, often in

Left: Another of the Beadle-bodied Leyland Tiger Cubs delivered in the late 1950s, No 1071 (RUF 71) of 1956, shows off the distinctive side mouldings of the style that suffered in contact with a Welsh mountainside.
John Bishop collection

long white dustcoats, would stand by their vehicles, drumming up trade, but Southdown drivers never seemed as aggressive as those of the independent firms, many of whom would accost passers-by in an effort to gain custom.

The coaches provided by these independents were usually of Bedford or, in later years, Ford manufacture, although there were exceptions. Southdown would usually field a selection of Duple- or Harrington-bodied Royal Tigers and Beadle-bodied Tiger Cubs. Occasionally one of the angular all-Leyland Royal Tigers would appear, and, less frequently, a Beadle-Commer integral, both types being normally allocated to express services.

It was not until the late 1950s that Southdown joined the band of lightweight coach operators, opting for Commer Avengers with two-stroke engines and bodies by Burlingham and Harrington. They were not a success, particularly the Burlingham examples, which spent much of their lives lurking in the dark corners of depots and yards. They did venture out from time to time, and on one memorable occasion, a Derby Day when most of the open-toppers had been sent on their annual pilgrimage to Epsom Downs, two of the Burlingham-bodied Commers were put to work on the service 97 from Eastbourne to the top of Beachy Head. The sound of these two climbing Sanatorium Hill had to be heard to be believed!

The image extended beyond the maintenance of the buses and coaches to the specification of the vehicles themselves. Barring a few exceptions vehicles were built to Southdown's own requirements, which often involved considerable modification to the bodywork. The Northern Counties bodywork fitted to the company's Leyland PD3s was a case in point. Apart from a few 'lookalikes' built for independents this style was unique to Southdown, and in the minds of many the 'Queen Mary' has become synonymous with the company.

The company was staid, almost old-fashioned in some of its preferences. For instance it continued to specify half-drop windows long after the sliding ventilator had become almost universal. The 'slider' was standard on Leyland's Farington body, but Southdown (along with Portsmouth Corporation) specified half-drops. In 1946, when new vehicles were in short supply and it was a case of taking what was available, Southdown received two batches of Leyland PS1s with ECW bodywork. They were fitted with ECW's standard sliding vents, but Southdown replaced these with spring-loaded half-drops, which I'm sure weren't as efficient. Five-bay construction (*i.e.* with five main windows on the lower deck) was another example. Southdown never actually had any four-bay double-deckers, apart from an experimental double-deck coach. When the Park Royal-bodied Guys and PD2s were delivered in 1955/6 Park Royal's standard body, as supplied to neighbours East Kent and Maidstone & District, had four windows per side. Southdown specified — and received — five!

Coaches too were very much Southdown's 'own'. The mouldings on the front and sides of the first Duple-bodied Leyland Royal Tigers were adopted as standard and applied, with some variations, to all coaches bought up to the end of the 1950s, by which time they would have looked incongruous on more modern designs. Thus the Beadle bodies on Southdown's Commer TS3s looked vastly different from the standard version on East Kent's AEC Reliances.

Right: Favourites with both authors were the Eastern Coach Works-bodied Leyland Tiger PS1s of 1947. Demoted from coach to bus work in 1955, they gained destination screens front and rear and mostly retained their dark-green roofs, which arguably improved their appearance. Pictured at Haywards Heath bus station on 5 June 1960 is the former 1231 (GUF 731), by now renumbered 687. *Gerald Mead*

Far right: Beadle having ceased its coachbuilding activities, Southdown turned to the Weymann Fanfare for the bodywork of its final Leyland Tiger Cubs, delivered in 1960. This attractive scene, recorded on 29 June 1966, features No 1138 (XUF 138) outside the Hydro Hotel, Paignton, while on a North & South Devon tour. *Gerald Mead*

Southdown
XUF 139

4. THE HUMAN FACTOR

If the company could not operate without its buses, the buses could not operate without its staff.

The Southdown image was perpetuated by the road staff — drivers, conductors and inspectors. Uniforms — jacket, trousers, tie, white shirt, black shoes and peaked cap — were obligatory, as, indeed, they were with most of the major operators. For anyone turning up for work improperly dressed there were penalties, the ultimate being to be sent home and lose a day's pay. Appearance was very highly placed on the list of priorities, and I remember when I was working for the company in 1959/60 a prospective driver coming for interview and being turned down because he had a beard. It has always seemed unfair to me that he was not given the true reason for his non-appointment – or the opportunity to shave off his beard, which he might well have willingly done. In summer grey linen jackets with green collars and cuffs were the order of the day, together with white covers on caps. If these weren't worn from the appropriate day, fines would, again, be imposed.

Bad timekeeping would also incur penalties, and anyone reporting for duty less than five minutes before the bus was due to depart would again be sent home and lose a day's pay. Inspectors — or 'jumpers', as they were known by the crews — would board buses without warning, checking that all passengers had tickets and had not travelled further than they should. The conductor's waybill would also be checked. This was a form that had to be completed at the end of each journey, giving the numbers of the last tickets issued and the amount collected. This was not too difficult in the days of the Setright and TIM machines, but in the era of Bell Punch tickets each denomination would have to be entered separately. If the tickets issued were not in order the conductor would be in trouble, and this could even lead to dismissal. However,

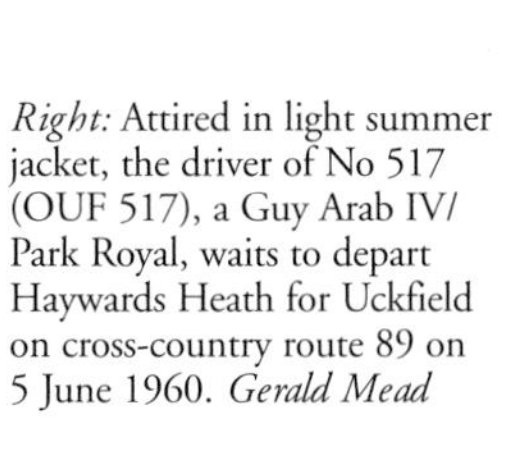
Right: Attired in light summer jacket, the driver of No 517 (OUF 517), a Guy Arab IV/ Park Royal, waits to depart Haywards Heath for Uckfield on cross-country route 89 on 5 June 1960. *Gerald Mead*

this did not prevent the more foolhardy from bucking the system by standing on the platform and collecting fares from upstairs passengers as they alighted, not issuing tickets and pocketing the takings. If a conductor were suspected of such behaviour a plain-clothes inspector would board the bus in an attempt to catch him red-handed, whereupon instant dismissal would result.

Although late running was frowned upon, the cardinal sin was running early, for this would result in passengers' being missed — and income lost. Perhaps surprisingly, timekeeping was the responsibility of the conductor, and it was up to him to delay ringing the bell at stops if he had a particularly eager driver. A conductor caught running early twice in one week would lose his 'good conduct' bonus. However, rules are made to be broken, and crews would use various tactics to make life easier. One such ploy was 'staircasing', which entailed running as close as possible behind the bus in front (especially if it belonged to another operator) so that its unfortunate crew would pick up all the passengers and do all the work!

Until the 1960s, when traffic began to decline, only a handful of lightly trafficked routes were worked by one-man operated buses, or 'one-man bands', as they were known, but, with falling passenger numbers and rising costs, one-man operation became almost universal. The eventual demise of the bus conductor was a sad loss, robbing us of some true characters, almost showmen. One I remember would shout "Room for four in the Circle and two in the Stalls!" whilst another would call out not only the name of the bus stop but everywhere within a half-mile radius. There were those that would sing or whistle, those that had what were almost catch-phrases such as "Hold very tight now" (in a very refined voice) or, when collecting fares, "I thangyou!", borrowed from comedian Arthur Askey. Most were ready with a quick retort; enquiries such as "Do you stop at the Pier?" would prompt the inevitable response "I hope so, madam — there'll be one heck of a splash if we don't!, while "How long will the next 12 be?" would be met with "About thirty feet, love — same as this one". However, I can never remember anyone taking offence. In those days most employees saw working 'on the buses' as a job for life – and were proud to do so. Many achieved their long-service awards, which were presented annually. It was a mutual arrangement, and the company took care of its staff. It had a thriving Sports Club, and employees' families were equally well catered for, with concessionary travel as well as Christmas parties and outings for the children.

Women were first employed as conductresses — or 'clippies' — during World War 2, when so many of Southdown's male employees had been called up to join the Forces. However, it was obvious that the company saw this as a strictly temporary measure. A letter from the company to a prospective 'clippie' written in 1941 stated:

Southdown Motor Services Limited

LONG SERVICE CERTIFICATE

Presented to

Alfred Sydney Tidey

upon the Completion of

TWENTY-FIVE YEARS

Loyal and Valued Service

Chairman

General Manager

Secretary

Date 26th May 1955

Left: Employees who completed 25 years' service with Southdown were, quite rightly, presented with a certificate recording the fact. Such was the case with Alfred Sydney Tidey, whose son, Robin, kindly made it available to be photographed. *John Bishop / Online Transport Archive*

Below: Long-service badge, as worn proudly by Alfred Tidey. *John Bishop / Online Transport Archive*

'With reference to your recent interview I beg to inform you that we have decided to employ you as a bus conductress, on a month's trial, starting on Wednesday 26th November 1941. As I informed you at the interview, the engagement will be of a purely temporary nature.'

Starting pay for this lady was four shillings (20p) per day plus 2½d (about 1p) an hour war wage; after four months this rose to 1s 2½d (6½p) per hour plus 21½d per hour war wage.

Right: With Duple-bodied Leyland Tiger PS1 No 1329 (HUF 929) as a backdrop, a group of fellow employees pose with Driver Marsh (centre) on the occasion of his retirement, in 1954. The retirement of a long-serving member of staff was a regarded as a significant event and was often featured in the local paper. *Worthing Gazette / John Bishop collection*

Far right: This copy of a painting by one of the authors has been published before but nevertheless warrants inclusion here, if only to portray the hustle and bustle typical of Brighton's Pool Valley bus station in the late 1950s. Its conductor poised to press the bell at the critical moment, all-Leyland PD2/12 No 728 (LUF 228) of 1951 reverses into the bay alongside PD2/1 No 318 (JCD 18) of 1948 (right), while on the left are 137 (BUF 237), a 1935 Titan TD4 rebodied potstwar by East Lancs, and 533 (PUF 633), a Guy Arab IV/ Park Royal new in 1956. *Glyn Kraemer-Johnson*

During the summer months many of the more experienced and longer-serving drivers would turn to coach work, and this, together with the increase in traffic brought about by the annual influx of holidaymakers, made it necessary for more staff to be employed. This shortfall was met partly by the employment of university students, and this in turn brought into the workforce some unlikely characters, on occasions even including the nobility.

As well as the regular duties there was also a 'spares list' at each depot, and drivers and conductors allocated to this would cover for sickness and holidays etc. At busy times (mainly weekends) engineers and fitters — in fact anyone holding a valid PSV licence — would be offered these duties on overtime.

Upon asking friends and neighbours what they remembered about Southdown, I was surprised by the number who cited Pool Valley bus station, in Brighton. This was host to all but a few local services, but the site was hardly ideal for a bus station. The procedure for arriving buses involved rounding the south side of the Old Steine and then pulling into the middle of the road to gain sufficient clearance on the nearside before swinging into the very narrow, downward-sloping road that formed the approach to Pool Valley. (Southdown seemed to have a predilection for bus and coach stations with tight entrances; Brighton's Steine Street coach station was another case in point, as was Pevensey Road in Eastbourne, where buses were required to negotiate a narrow tunnel leading into the bus station.) In the 'Valley' itself an inspector would indicate to the driver where he should park. If the bus was to be changed or subject to a lengthy layover it would be parked on the side adjacent to the Savoy cinema; if it was to go straight out again on service it would reverse into the appropriate bay, and this was the exercise that was fascinating to watch. The pavement was laid out in a saw-tooth pattern, each bay being dedicated to one or more services. The driver would line up his bus with the relevant bay and reverse slowly, still with all his passengers on board, into the bay, frequently between two other vehicles. The conductor would hang off the rear platform, one finger poised over the bell push. As the rear wheels came to the edge of the pavement he would ring the bell, and the bus would come to a standstill.

Of course, with the advent of front- or forward-entrance vehicles, of up to 36ft in length, entry into the 'Valley' and reversing into the bay became increasingly difficult, and, in addition, it was necessary for passengers to squeeze between the buses when boarding or alighting. From the 1970s services were progressively diverted to terminate at the Churchill Square shopping centre, and today Pool Valley serves primarily as an express-coach station (Steine Street having closed in the early 1970s), the level of activity being but a faint echo of that witnessed in its heyday.

YE
OLDE
12
SALTDEAN
PEACEHAVEN
NEWHAVEN
SEAFORD
LITTLEWOODS
SOUTHDOWN
LUF 228
25 EASTBOURNE
17 HORSHAM
BUF 237
PUF 633
119
Johnson
1995

5. SOUTHDOWN REMEMBERED

Notwithstanding the aforementioned school trip on the lowbridge Guy, my first regular experience of travelling by Southdown came in 1949, when my father spent six months in Southlands Hospital, Shoreham, and naturally my mother wanted to visit him every day. At that time we lived in Hangleton, West Hove, and the daily journey to the hospital, involving three buses each way, was an enthusiast's dream. From Hangleton to Portslade on route 8 our regular bus was one of Brighton, Hove & District's two Pickering-bodied utility Guys, still with wooden seats. At Portslade a change was made to BH&D route 2, on which the bus would be a prewar Bristol K5G with ECW body finished by BH&D. Then came the *pièce de résistance*: from the BH&D boundary at Kingston Lane to the hospital we would travel by Southdown service 21, worked by one of the beautiful '1400'-class single-deckers. These were Leyland TS7s and TS8s, with rear-entrance Harrington bodywork, built between 1935 and 1939. Maidstone & District had some that looked similar, but the '1400s' were very much Southdown's 'own'. They were equipped with comprehensive destination displays consisting of a full-size screen (as fitted to double-deckers) at the front and below the rear window, while on the nearside was a full display comprising three boxes for the ultimate destination, intermediate points and, between them, the route number. During the war most had been converted as 'standee' vehicles with perimeter seating, but by 1949 they had regained their original semi-coach seats. Unfortunately the journey from Kingston Lane to Southlands Hospital was not long enough to savour the finer points of these magnificent machines, but the growl of the Tiger has stayed with me ever since. What a disappointment that none survived to be preserved.

Of course, this was in the days when Matron ruled, and visiting was restricted to an hour each evening and two hours on Wednesday and Sunday afternoons. A number of hospitals in the Sussex area were not easily accessible by public transport, so Southdown operated special Hospital services to Hellingly Hospital, Robertsbridge Sanatorium and Cuckfield Hospital, as well as Southlands. These were timed to arrive at the hospital at the start of visiting time and depart when it ended – and both patients and visitors heaved a sigh of relief!

My father was a member of the British Legion, and it was around this time that my mother and I were invited to join their annual outing – a river cruise from Richmond to Hampton Court. The vehicle provided for the journey was, as I recall, one of Southdown's normal-control Leyland Cubs. It was a particularly hot July day, and we experienced the novelty of travelling with the canvas roof folded back. On the way home we stopped at a hostelry and, as was customary for children in those days, I stood outside with a packet of crisps and my first-ever glass of Cola, fascinated by the drummer of a band that was playing just inside the open door. Whether it was the heat, the excitement, the Cola or (most unlikely) the fumes from the engine I don't know, but I was violently sick all the way home. I was not a popular child!

Below: The clean lines of the Harrington-bodied Leyland Tiger TS8 – as used on route 21 between Brighton and Shoreham Beach – are apparent from this view of No 1479 (GCD 379) on Hurstpierpoint local service 34. Regrettably none survived to be preserved, many ending their days as chicken houses and farm outbuildings after their mechanical components had been salvaged for reuse in chassisless Beadle coaches or to re-power petrol-engined Titans for Eastbourne Corporation. *John Bishop collection*

This reminds me of a friend who suffered from the same complaint but on a more regular basis. He lived on Hayling Island and went to school in Emsworth, travelling every day on one of the little Dennis Falcons bought specifically for the Hayling Island service. Unfortunately every morning without fail he would be ill, and eventually Southdown arranged for a spare vehicle to be waiting at Havant every schoolday morning!

In 1951 my schooling moved to Seaford, and I was obliged to go as a boarder. This was deep in Southdown territory, but for the next two years I saw nothing but JCD-registered all-Leyland PD2/1s on the 12 and Leyland and Park Royal-bodied PD1s on the 123 from Haywards Heath; '1400s' also ran into Seaford, but I can't recall ever seeing one. Then again, we were confined to the school grounds except for a twice-weekly walk, on Wednesday and Saturday afternoons, and that usually took us away from the town rather than towards it. No, it wasn't a borstal — it just seemed like it! And I was missing so much that was going on back in Brighton, notably the first 8ft-wide double-deckers and the first underfloor-engined coaches and single-deckers. The first I knew about underfloor-engined vehicles was when my mother bought me a Dinky Toys model of a Duple Roadmaster coach. It looked so futuristic I didn't believe it was based on a real coach!

But I made up for it during the holidays. By this time we had moved to the Lewes Road area of Brighton, which was served by BH&D, Brighton Corporation buses and trolleybuses and, at an extra charge, Southdown. Not only did Southdown charge higher fares; its buses stopped less frequently, and where they did share the same stopping-place they had a separate stop sign a few yards away from that of the local operators. This was obviously all part of the protection scheme, but it created the impression that the company didn't want to be associated with BH&D and the Corporation.

Southdown's routes along Lewes Road consisted of all the country services to Lewes and beyond, which provided a combined 10-minute headway, and the local services to Coldean, Moulsecoomb and Bevendean, which were operated almost exclusively by utility Guys. By now the Guys had been modified and brought up to peacetime standard, and to the average passenger one of these was probably 'just another Southdown bus' although the throbbing Gardner engine and typical Guy whistle were something of a giveaway. Some of the all-Leyland PD2/1s, displaced from the front-line coastal services 12 and 31, were beginning to appear on the longer inland routes, but in the main these were still handled by prewar Leyland TDs. In the late 1940s Southdown had embarked on a massive programme of rebodying prewar 'deckers, which was carried out by the usual builders – Park Royal, East Lancs, Northern Counties and Beadle — as well as Saunders. This gave Southdown a fleet of around 150 prewar buses that were nearly as good as new and quite capable of handling most of the country services. It also ensured that the familiar growl of the Leyland 8.6-litre engine would be heard throughout the area into the 1960s.

In 1953 I returned to school in Brighton and for the next few years witnessed the delivery of what I now see as British buses at the peak of their design — Leyland PD2/12s with bodies variously by Leyland itself, Northern Counties, Park Royal, Beadle and East Lancs, the last very definitely the *crème de la crème*. I remember 1 January 1957, when a schoolfriend and I had arranged to meet four girls. (I can't imagine why there were four; I wasn't usually that lucky!) As we walked around the Old Steine I suggested taking a quick look in Pool Valley, and there, pristine and gleaming, was a brand-new East Lancs-bodied PD2.

Left: Professing an interest in old buses can elicit material from the most unexpected source, and during his time in the employ of Sussex Police the writer was delighted to be presented with this photograph of 1936 Leyland Titan TD4 No 144 (CCD 944), with lowbridge Beadle bodywork, impaled on the corner of Market Street in Lewes. Although undated it is likely to have been taken in the 1950s, judging from the lining on the roof and the fact that the image is derived from a glass negative. *Sussex Police / John Bishop collection*

Above: In 1946 Southdown embarked upon an extensive programme of rebodying prewar Leyland Titans. TD5 No 158 (EUF 158), new in 1938 with a lowbridge Park Royal body, was rebodied 10 years later by Beadle to this rather dated six-bay style. It is seen waiting to depart Brighton's Pool Valley bus station on the lengthy 122 route to Gravesend, Kent, a journey that would take just under four hours. Note the autovac (for the fuel delivery) on the nearside bulkhead; also that the radiator grille and surround are painted dark green. *W. J. Haynes*

I surveyed it from every angle, climbed on board, savouring the smell of fresh paint, new leather and upholstery, then got off again and stood staring at it, open-mouthed and quite oblivious of my friend's impatiently shuffling feet. I had never seen anything quite so beautiful. Eventually the engine purred into life, and the bus pulled out onto the seafront and headed off westward at the start of its long journey to Portsmouth. Absently I followed my friend to the coffee bar, where we had arranged to meet the girls. They didn't stand a chance – they couldn't hold a candle to that PD2!

Obviously impressed with the performance and reliability of the wartime Guys (many of which were now being converted into open-toppers) and of a dozen Northern Counties-bodied Arab IIIs received in 1948/9, Southdown purchased no fewer than 48 Arab IVs in 1955/6. (For some reason the company usually bought its buses in multiples of 12.) They had handsome Park Royal bodies which in terms of appearance owed more than a little to the London RT, although the second batch introduced Southdown to the sliding window, which somehow gave these vehicles a much sleeker appearance.

By the mid-1950s Leyland Royal Tigers with distinctive but not particularly attractive bodies by East Lancs had replaced my beloved '1400s'. However, they were very comfortable and, being of centre- or rear-entrance layout, had the added advantage of enabling you to sit next to the driver. Unfortunately this was an asset that disappeared when they were all converted to front-entrance for one-man operation.

Much is heard today of truancy amongst schoolchildren who frequent amusement arcades and the like, playing fruit machines, smoking, drinking and taking drugs. I must confess that I did my share of 'skipping off school', but I didn't gamble, drink or smoke pot – I used to go for bus rides. How sad is that? I travelled at some time or other on most of Brighton's country services. Only once did I ride on the 31 to Portsmouth and back. I found the journey particularly boring, the West Sussex coastal strip being flat and uninteresting; indeed, I find the comparable train journey much the same today. I did, however, have a couple of favourite jaunts. One was the 122 to Gravesend, which was actually a few minutes longer than the 31 but passed through some picturesque villages and glorious countryside. And once Tunbridge Wells was reached the route ran along the boundary between Maidstone & District and London Transport, so there were vehicles of both operators to be seen. At the time of my wanderings both Southdown and Maidstone & District were using all-Leyland PD2/12s on the route (M&D's being inferior, of course!). Also appearing quite regularly were M&D's *very* inferior PD2/12s with Weymann Orion bodies, whilst Southdown was beginning to allocate PD2/12s with the sumptuous East Lancs bodies. What a contrast!

On a few occasions instead of returning by 122 I caught a Green Line RF on the 701 or 702 to Victoria and returned to Brighton on the London–Brighton express. Since the war the express services had been worked successively by ECW-bodied PS1s and all-Leyland Royal Tigers and were now in the hands of the Beadle-Commer integrals (Nos 1-25). I loved these machines, possibly because I've always tended to favour the uncommon and because with their rasping exhausts they sounded a bit like Bristol Ks – noisy but full of character. In addition they were built in Dartford, my birthplace, and before the war my father had worked for Beadle as a storekeeper, so the coachbuilder had always been a little bit special.

The year 1957 was a good one, for as well as drooling over brand-new PD2s I spent a fortnight with my grandmother, who still lived in Dartford. One afternoon I was waiting at the bus stop outside her house for the inevitable RT when I heard a familiar and unmistakable sound in the distance. No RT, this, but Southdown's Beadle-Commer 21 (TUF 21) in undercoat, presumably undergoing a test run. *Why* didn't I have a camera with me?

When new the integrals carried the Beadle badge on the front panel. It was an attractive emblem consisting of a white shield on which was the prancing horse of Kent, in red. Sadly, along with the Royal Tiger and Tiger Cub badges, they were replaced by Southdown's own, an apple-green triangle with '*Southdown*' in yellow script. It added individuality and was all part of the image, but it always seemed rather unfair that the chassis manufacturer's name should be removed, especially on an underfloor-engined single-decker, on which the only remaining identification was on the wheel hubs. I think that the Guy double-deckers were probably the only vehicles to escape such treatment.

On one very memorable occasion I was returning to Brighton by express coach from (I think) a visit to the Commercial Motor Show at Earl's Court, my steed being Southdown Beadle-Commer No 1 (RUF 101). Just south of Handcross the coach shuddered to a halt. The driver got out — needless to say it was dark and raining — and, on his return a few minutes later, asked: "Can anyone drive one of these?" Silence. "I just want someone to rev it up for me." "I'll do it! I'll do it!" I cried, pushing my way towards the front of the coach in case anyone else got there first. And there I sat, a 16-year-old schoolboy in the driving seat of a fully laden Beadle-Commer, gently revving the engine. As I've already said, I loved the sound of these machines, especially when they were accelerating, so I gave it a bit more 'welly' — then a bit more, until the driver gently eased me from the seat. "Ball bearings all over the bloody road," he said, so we had to wait for Brighton to send a Tiger Cub to the rescue.

Beadle-Commers used also to feature in my Friday evenings out. Getting drunk? Nightclubbing? Not on your life. I used to spend them at Southdown's Steine Street coach station. (I did tell you I was sad!) This was another of Southdown's barely accessible sites. Coaches entered by the narrow Manchester Street, a turning off busy St James's Street, the latter being two-way in those days, even with trolleybuses running in both directions. The coach station itself had space for about three or four coaches, with another three parked up. There was also a small 'auxiliary' garage on the opposite side of the road with space for another four or so. On busy summer Saturdays, when a steady stream of coaches were waiting to enter the coach station, they would queue up in Manchester Street and in St James's Street itself, causing chaos! On Friday evenings, however, it was quiet. There would be the usual hourly London Express departures, the last leaving at 9pm, although coaches travelling into Brighton would continue to arrive at half past the hour until 10.30pm. Meanwhile, at 7.30pm, a Royal Blue Bristol LS or MW would arrive from Bournemouth on the South Coast Express, and the Station Inspector would change the antimacassars before it headed back to Portsmouth at 8pm. At about the same time a Willowbrook Viking-bodied AEC Reliance in the smart maroon, grey and cream livery of Grey Cars would arrive from Totnes, a journey that would have taken some 10 hours. At 8.15pm another of my favourites would arrive from Cheltenham in the shape of a Willowbrook-bodied Guy Arab LUF belonging to Black & White Motorways; I always wanted to ride on one of these handsome machines but never did. Then, at 9.50, came the highlight of the evening – a Beadle-Commer Rochester in the red and cream livery of Yorkshire Woollen District, which had left Harrogate exactly 12 hours previously. Once it had been safely parked in the corner of the coach station I knew it was time to head for home. And what did I do between these arrivals and departures? I stood outside the pub next to the coach station, listening to the jukebox. One record in particular sticks in my mind — 'Jacqueline' by Bobby Helms, no doubt because I was in love with a girl called Jacqueline at the time. I don't know what she'd have thought if she'd known how I spent my Friday evenings!

Back to my schoolday jaunts, and one which was probably my favourite. This was to catch a 25 from Brighton to Eastbourne via Lewes and Polegate, returning along the coast road on a 12. There were still a few prewar Leylands on the inland country routes, but in the main these were worked by the Park Royal-bodied Guy Arab IVs of 1955/6. Lovely vehicles, these were spoiled only by the ridiculously high front-bulkhead windows; presumably designed for the AEC Regent V, they looked completely out of place on the Arab IV, with its low bonnet line. Once past Lewes, when stops and passengers were few and far between, the Guys would purr along contentedly, giving the impression that, were it not for the water in between, they would have happily carried on until they reached Hong Kong, which was where most of them ended their days. I remember the Area Engineer at Brighton telling me that you could put a Gardner 6LW into a Guy and forget about it.

At Eastbourne I would leave the Guy, certain that these were the best 'deckers in the Southdown fleet. Then I would travel back to Brighton on a PD2/12 with Beadle or East Lancs bodywork, wondering '... or are they?' Even today I find myself unable to choose between preserved PD2/Beadle 786, PD2/East Lancs 805 and Arab/Park Royal 547. Whatever, they represent British bus design at its very zenith.

Right: In the period 1946-50 no fewer than five bodybuilders were engaged to build new bodies for prewar Titans, the buses in question being TD3s, TD4s and TD5s delivered in the years 1934-9. New in 1938 with a lowbridge Park Royal body, No 174 (EUF 174) was in 1949 rebodied by the same builder to highbridge style, being seen thus at Haywards Heath bus station on 5 June 1960. *Gerald Mead*

Right: The postwar bodies produced by Beadle, especially the six-bay versions, looked dated in comparison with contemporary styles from other builders. Making the point in this attractive scene at the Carfax, Horsham, is TD5 No 155 (EUF 155), new in 1938 with lowbridge Park Royal bodywork. Note also the dark-green lining above and below the windows, as well as Southdown's curious habit of placing the registration plate above the cab rather than in its 'proper place' below the radiator.
John Bishop collection

Top left: Very much in the minority among the builders employed in the rebodying programme was Saunders, which bodied just nine chassis, in 1947. Among these was TD4 No 117 (BUF 217), new in 1935 as a 'gearless' TD4c with highbridge Short Bros bodywork (see page 18) and pictured in Felpham on a Bognor Regis local service on 22 February 1949. Close scrutiny of the offside aft of the rear wheel-arch reveals the 'H' suffix beneath the fleet number, indicating this to be a highbridge vehicle.
J. Cull / The Omnibus Society

Above: Of all the body styles used to rebody the prewar Titans the most handsome (as well as the most numerous) was surely that produced by East Lancs. Among the 60 chassis so fitted was that of TD5 No 207 (FCD 507), new in 1939 with Park Royal body. Looking immaculate with dark-green lining, the bus is seen in Chichester shortly after rebodying in 1949, at a time when hats were a natural part of everyday dress. *Eric Surfleet / Southdown Enthusiasts' Club*

Left: The final bodybuilder to participate in the rebodying programme was Northern Counties, which in 1950 bodied 17 chassis to this distinctive style. Seen at Haywards Heath bus station on the same date as No 174 *opposite top* is No 154 (DUF 154), a Leyland TD5 that had been new in 1937 with a highbridge Park Royal body. *Gerald Mead*

Right: New in 1939 with Park Royal bodywork but rebodied by Northern Counties in 1950, Leyland TD5 No 254 (GCD 354) was captured on 2 February 1957 at Paulsgrove while on Portsmouth on city service 21. Note that by this time it had received a separate route-number box, here being used to inform intending passengers that the 21 served Hilsea Lido – not that the weather appears entirely suitable! *John Bishop collection*

Below: A Leyland Titan TD4 dating from 1935 and rebodied postwar by East Lancs, 129 (BUF 229) speeds past Southsea Common on its way to South Parade Pier. Note the fine condition of the City of Portsmouth trolleybus wiring, which by the time of this photograph, taken in the late 1950s, contrasted with that of many other trolleybus systems. *Phil Tatt / Online Transport Archive*

Far right: New in 1938, Leyland Titan TD5 No 163 (EUF 163) was rebodied postwar by Beadle but looks positively antiquated in this photograph, taken at Southsea in the late 1950s. Nevertheless, fresh out of the paint shop it shows just what could be achieved with a fine livery applied by skilled staff. In the background is South Parade Pier, which in later years would be severely damaged in an horrendous fire. *Phil Tatt / Online Transport Archive*

43
BEDHAMPTON
HAVANT
WESTBOURNE
(FOR COMPTON)
EUF 163
'Wonderloaf'
SOUTHDOWN

Right: In 1956 a new bus station and garage opened in Chichester. Hitherto buses had terminated outside the Cathedral in West Street, which thoroughfare was also the location of the enquiry office, but the new facility provided a perfect interchange for travellers, being adjacent to the railway station. Dating from 30 September 1956, this splendid panorama was recorded from the garage forecourt, the station footbridge being just visible on the left. *Bruce Jenkins*

Right: The simplified lines of the postwar Park Royal body mounted on Leyland Titan TD5 No 233 (FUF 233) are seen to their best advantage in this nearside view at Chichester. The absence of lining dates the photograph to the late 1950s, by which time the livery had been simplified as an economy measure. Note the fuel 'autovac' located alongside the engine, below the front bulkhead window. *Phil Tatt / Online Transport Archive*

Left: As a young 'bus spotter' one would often gain access to the various Southdown garages in the hope of seeing the unusual or rare bus or coach. Invariably the older vehicles would be resting after their peak-hour duties, as was the case with these two 1938 Leyland Titan TD5s inside Chichester depot in June 1961. Both had been rebodied postwar, 237 (FUF 237), on the left, by East Lancs, and 209 (FCD 509) by Northern Counties. No 237 illustrates Southdown's curious practice of affixing the registration plate between the decks, despite the fact that provision is made below the radiator grille. *Bruce Jenkins*

Left: In the early 1960s many Southdown vehicles met their end in Light's scrapyard at Southerham, near Lewes. Enthusiasts were often denied access, causing much frustration, but with the right approach the photographer was able to record this sorry scene featuring 1937 Leyland Titan TD5 No 151 (DUF 151), rebodied postwar by East Lancs, with a Brighton trolleybus behind. *John Bishop / Online Transport Archive*

Right: The first of the wartime Guy Arabs, delivered in 1943, lowbridge Northern Counties-bodied 400 (GCD 974) shows off its angular and functional lines on a warm day in postwar Brighton as it awaits departure from Pool Valley on local service 13B to North Moulscombe (this being the spelling adopted by Southdown, as opposed to the 'Moulsecoomb' that has since been generally accepted). In common with a number of others of its type this vehicle would later be given a marginally newer East Lancs utility body (used initially to rebody a prewar Leyland TD2), in which form it would soldier on into the early 1960s – which shows just how good the mechanicals were, despite the utility specification.
W. J. Haynes / Southdown Enthusiasts' Club

Right: In full Southdown livery, complete with dark-green lining, even wartime utility bodywork begins to look attractive! Pictured in Brighton's Old Steine in the late 1950s, Weymann-bodied 490 (GUF 390) is passed by a Brighton Corporation AEC Regent – also bodied by Weymann, but to peacetime specification.
Eric Surfleet / Southdown Enthusiasts' Club

Left: From 1950 a significant proportion of the wartime Guy Arabs were converted to open-top, in which form they could in the summer months be found almost anywhere along the coast between Portsmouth and Eastbourne. Representing one of the earlier conversions, having been completed in the spring of 1951, Park Royal-bodied No 442 (GUF 142) is seen on a glorious summer's day on Hayling Island. *Eric Surfleet / Southdown Enthusiasts' Club*

Left: The later open-top conversions of utility Guy Arabs were perhaps less pleasing in appearance than the earlier examples, although with dark-green lining and coach-style scroll fleetnames they still had the Southdown 'sparkle'. Seen in Pool Valley, Brighton, on 7 August 1961, Northern Counties-bodied 421 (GUF 121) displays a 'lazy' blind for route 27 to Devil's Dyke. *Gerald Mead*

Right: A busy scene at Eastbourne's Pevensey Road bus station in the early postwar period, with Northern Counties-bodied Guy Arab No 457 (GUF 157) preparing to depart on the circular route to Polegate. Note the black patch on the arm of the lady on the left of the picture, worn as a mark of respect for a fallen loved one. *The Omnibus Society*

Below: Resplendent in its revised livery following conversion to open-top in July 1950, Park Royal-bodied Guy Arab 409 (GUF 69) makes an interesting comparison with the previous generation of open-toppers, Brush-bodied Leyland Titan TD1s of 1929, represented in this official view by No 817 (UF 4817). *Alan Lambert collection*

Below right: Open-top conversion of Guy Arabs continued throughout the 1950s, later examples being used to replace earlier conversions. Among the last so treated, in April 1959, was Northern Counties-bodied 419 (GUF 119), seen here at Beachy Head in August 1961. *Bruce Jenkins*

Above: A superb 'picture postcard' view of open-top Park Royal-bodied Guy Arab 496 (GUF 396) heading for Beachy Head past the carpet gardens in Eastbourne, with a similar vehicle just visible in the background. The pair represent the earliest open-top conversions by Southdown, the mouldings around the destination screen adding that little extra something for so long associated with the Southdown fleet. *Phil Tatt / Online Transport Archive*

Above: In 1946 Southdown took its first delivery of peacetime buses in the form of 25 Leyland Titan PD1s, although the bodywork, by Park Royal, was still to semi-utility design, while the Leyland E181 engine, developed from wartime use in military vehicles, had a very slow tickover, to the extent that one expected it to stall at any moment! However, these were very sturdy vehicles that would stand the test of time, No 274 (GUF 674) being seen on Worthing seafront in the early 1960s. Drawn up on the beach behind is a typical Sussex clinker boat, with 'SM' (Shoreham) registration. *John Bishop*

Right: The second postwar delivery of double-deckers, received in 1947, comprised 25 all-Leyland PD1s to a more relaxed specification. These too had long lives, those in the Brighton and Worthing areas being found latterly on routes 9 and, as here, 10, on which No 304 (HCD 904) is seen departing Pool Valley. The photograph is undated but would appear to have been taken in the early 1960s, judging from the presence in the Old Steine of a forward-entrance Brighton Corporation PD2. *John Bishop collection*

Left: The largest single batch of vehicles delivered to Southdown consisted of no fewer than 80 all-Leyland PD2/1s received in 1948. The main difference from the earlier PD1 model lay in the mechanics, specifically the new O.600 engine and synchromesh gearbox. No 391 (JCD 91) is seen at Worthing garage on 23 September 1962, at which time televisions were often rented rather than bought. *Gerald Mead*

Left: Crash gearboxes notwithstanding, the wartime Guy Arabs continued to give valuable service into the 1960s, in both open- and closed-top form. This 1959 view inside Worthing garage features Northern Counties-bodied No 418 (GUF 118) alongside 372 (JCD 72), another of the all-Leyland PD2/1s of 1948. *John Bishop / Online Transport Archive*

Right: Taken at the village of East Dean, near Eastbourne, this delightful family portrait has as its backdrop all-Leyland PD2/1 No 332 (JCD 32), setting down passengers on its way to Brighton. The photograph is undated but was presumably taken in the spring of 1948, when the bus was new, and permits a study of the rear aspect of this nicely proportioned design. Note also the 'H' (highbridge) suffix to the fleet number, just visible to the left of the rear wheel-arch. *John Bishop collection*

Right: Enabling its handsome lines to be appreciated from a more conventional angle, all-Leyland PD2/1 No 338 (JCD 38) turns onto the main road at Shoreham-by-Sea on 22 September 1962. By this time, however, economies were being implemented with regard to the livery, and comparison with the previous photograph reveals a simplified version without dark-green lining. *Gerald Mead*

Left: The rebodied prewar Titans survived into the early 1960s. This varied line-up, recorded *c*1960 at Hilsea garage, features TD5s Nos 223 (FUF 223) and 254 (GCD 354), dating from 1939 and rebodied postwar by Park Royal and Northern Counties respectively, flanking Northern Counties-bodied Guy Arab III No 507 of 1949, while just in view on the left is Leyland PD3/Northern Counties 846 (XUF 846), new in 1959 and still retaining its rear destination display, the use of which would shortly be abandoned. *John Bishop*

Left: Another line-up, this time along the coast at Bognor Regis and showing the progression of Leyland Titan design. From left to right are 1939 TD5 No 208 (FCD 508), with postwar East Lancs body, Park Royal-bodied PD1 No 289 (GUF 689) of 1946 and all-Leyland PD2/1 No 388 (JCD 88) of 1948. Many readers will also have fond memories of the Morris 8, an example of which is partly visible on the right. *John Bishop / Online Transport Archive*

HAVANT
TRUSTEE SAVINGS
BANK
SOUTHDOWN
LONDON
Southdown

Far left: Surprising survivors in the 1950s were a number of the prewar Leyland Cubs, which owed their continued existence to the weak Langstone Bridge linking Hayling Island with the mainland. This photograph was taken at Havant railway station on 26 August 1956, on the occasion of a Southdown Enthusiasts' Club tour.
Bruce Jenkins

Left: Delivered in 1949 for services to and from Hayling Island were ten 30-seat Dennis Falcons, among them No 90 (JCD 90), seen when new at Havant on 28 September. Although the bodywork was by Dennis these vehicles were similar to an earlier Harrington-bodied pair, delivered in 1939, and in this view one cannot help but notice a distinct likeness to the prewar Tiger buses ('1400s') bodied by the same builder.
J. Cull / The Omnibus Society

Bottom: A later view at Havant, featuring Dennis Falcon No 86 (JUF 86) on layover between journeys to and from Hayling Island. Older readers will doubtless recall a time when passengers had to alight and walk across the Langstone Bridge because of the weight restrictions – a requirement that ceased in the late 1950s following the construction of a new bridge.
Bruce Jenkins

Right: In the postwar years Southdown continued to favour Leyland for its coaching requirements, choosing the Leyland Tiger PS1 chassis, which was similar to the PD1 double-deck bus chassis. Included in the 1947 deliveries were 25 with functional yet handsome 31-seat bodywork by Eastern Coach Works, represented here by No 1242 (GUF 742). In the mid-1950s these vehicles would be downgraded as very comfortable service buses, as illustrated on page 26. *The Omnibus Society*

Right: Of the postwar Leyland Tiger PS1 coaches Harrington, surprisingly, bodied just six, and these and a similar number of Windover-bodied vehicles were the only examples with forward entrances. Harrington-bodied No 1264 (HUF 4) is seen on South Parade, Southsea, on 4 October 1948. *J. Cull / The Omnibus Society*

Left: Completing the 1947 delivery of Leyland PS1 coaches were the six Windover-bodied examples, easily distinguishable by the decorative sweeps behind the wheels and represented here by 1273 (HUF 273) at Southsea. *John Bishop collection*

Left: Further PS1s arrived in 1948/9, bodied by Beadle, Park Royal and Duple, bringing to 125 the number of this type operated. However, the advent of the underfloor-engined coach left half-cabs looking old-fashioned, and in the early 1950s the Duple- and Beadle-bodied PS1s were rebuilt with full fronts by the Dartford builder, modernising their appearance, although the removal of the front bulkhead inevitably increased engine noise in the saloon. This view inside Brighton's Freshfield Road garage features Beadle-bodied 1288 (HUF 288) alongside another rebuild from the same source in the form of chassisless Beadle-Leyland 859 (LCD 859), constructed in 1952 using running units from a prewar TS8. *John Bishop / Online Transport Archive*

WEST STREET MOTORS LTD
OFFICIAL ROOTES GROUP DEALER
Phone... EAST GRINSTEAD 3841 (10 LINES)
ALWAYS HAVE 150 to 200 CARS
& COMMERCIAL VEHICLES IN STOCK
SUN VALLEY TOBACCO
SALTDEAN
PEACEHAVEN
NEWHAVEN
SEAFORD
SUN VALLEY TOBACCO
LUF 234
SOUTHDOWN

Far left: This fine study of all-Leyland PD2 No 734 (LUF 234), recorded on Brighton seafront on 19 April 1959, shows to good advantage the 8ft width of these vehicles. New in 1952, this was one of the first to be delivered with platform doors already fitted – a development which, in the opinion of this writer, did nothing to enhance an otherwise attractive design. Sadly Leyland's bodybuilding activities would cease two years later, compelling Southdown to look elsewhere. *Gerald Mead*

Left: Upon withdrawal in the early 1950s many of the prewar Leyland TS7s and TS8s had their mechanical units salvaged to be reused by Beadle in the construction of modern-looking full-front 'chassisless' vehicles, including 26-seat coach 871 (MCD 871), 'new' in 1953. This particular vehicle, renumbered 650, would be one of 10 demoted to stage-carriage work in 1957/8, of which similar 649 (MUF 488), formerly 888, survives today in preservation.
Glyn Kraemer-Johnson collection

Left: Southdown's first truly modern coaches, with engines mounted under the floor, had arrived in 1951 in the form of 10 Duple-bodied Leyland Royal Tigers, and in the years that followed these were joined by further examples bodied by Duple, Harrington and Leyland itself. One of the later Duple-bodied coaches, No 1672 (NUF 72) of 1953, was photographed at Wembley in April 1954. The distinctive mouldings, relieving the livery of all-over green, would be a Southdown hallmark for a decade. *Bruce Jenkins*

Right: The East Lancs-bodied Leyland Royal Tiger saloons numbered 40 vehicles, an initial batch of 10 rear-entrance examples delivered in 1952 being followed in 1953 by 30 centre-entrance versions. Seen at Pool Valley, Brighton, in May 1956 is 1510 (MCD 510), numerically the first of the centre-entrance variety. *Bruce Jenkins*

Right: Another of the 1953 batch of Leyland Royal Tiger buses, No 1537 (MCD 537), waits time in Arundel's small bus station (long since redeveloped) before making the short journey to the nearby village of Burpham. These vehicles were designed to be worked by a conductor, but in the late 1950s, with the spread of one-man operation, all 40 would be converted to front-entrance layout, thereby denying passengers the chance to sit at the front alongside the driver. *John Bishop collection*

Left: The Royal Tigers were followed from 1954 by Tiger Cubs, which in terms of livery had all the refinements one would expect from Southdown, including dark-green roof and wheels, but the lighter-weight construction of the chassis resulted in greater noise intrusion from the underfloor engine. Photographed in Chichester bus station in the late 1950s, No 635 (MUF 635) was one of the first batch, bodied by Nudd Bros & Lockyer. As an interesting aside, Sussex has two villages named East Dean, this one being a little way north of Chichester, the other some 50 miles away, between Seaford and Eastbourne. *Phil Tatt / Online Transport Archive*

Left: A further five Tiger Cubs, delivered in 1955, were bodied by Park Royal, among them 641 (OUF 641), the subject of this official photograph. Although the design is little more than a square box (to paraphrase the comments of many a passenger), the combination of mouldings, brightwork and, of course, Southdown's livery application give this the air of a quality product. *Park Royal Vehicles / Glyn Kraemer-Johnson collection*

Right: The cessation of Leyland's bodybuilding activities forced Southdown to look elsewhere, and the 1955 batch of Leyland PD2/12s received this very attractive Park Royal design, which owed much to the style developed for the London Transport RT. Seen in Lewes Road, Brighton, on local service 38, No 772 (OCD 772) would survive to be preserved following an extended career with the company as a driver trainer. *Gerald Mead*

Right: Also bodied by Park Royal were 48 Guy Arab IVs, delivered in two batches in 1955/6. One of the second batch, No 535 (PUF 635) is seen in Haywards Heath on 26 April 1964 on the lengthy 89 route from Horsham to Uckfield. *Gerald Mead*

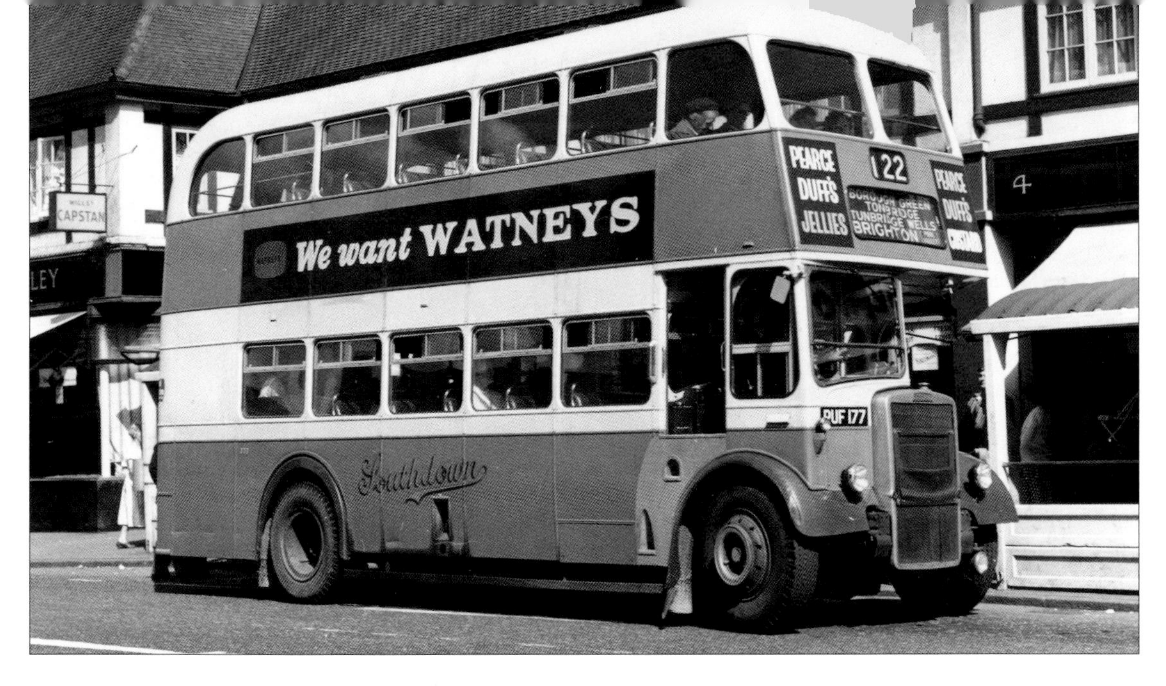

Left: Twelve Leyland PD2/12s delivered in 1956 would prove to be Southdown's last double-deckers bodied by Beadle, for by the end of the decade it too had withdrawn from the market. The similarity to the contemporary Park Royal design was no coincidence, for these bodies were built on Park Royal frames, but the interior finish was pure Beadle. No 777 (RUF 177), the first of the batch, is seen at Tonbridge, Kent, on 14 May 1960, with a long way still to go before reaching Brighton. Note the scroll fleetname, more readily associated with the coach fleet. *Gerald Mead*

Left: In the eyes of many the final Leyland Titan PD2/12s, bodied by East Lancs and delivered in 1956/7, were the most handsome of all. Seen in Uckfield bus station on 17 June 1962, No 809 (RUF 209) is about to resume its journey on service 122 to Gravesend, during which upper-deck passengers will be afforded a grandstand view of the Ashdown Forest. *Gerald Mead*

6. SOUTHDOWN AT WORK

In 1957 I applied for and was granted an apprenticeship with Thomas Harrington, the Hove coachbuilder, After a lot of thought I decided it would probably be more beneficial to stay on at school for another couple of years and improve my qualifications. In view of what subsequently happened to Harrington's, not to mention my utter inability to hang a picture, let alone build a coach, it was probably the right decision.

So I stayed on at school, took some more GCEs, failed most of them, enjoyed some more bus trips and, in 1959, applied for a position with Southdown, being duly accepted as a trainee on the three-year Management Training Scheme. I was given my free pass, enabling me to travel *gratis* to and from work, and my privilege ticket (or 'priv') that allowed me to travel for quarter fare at other times. My starting wage was £5 10s 0d (£5.50) per week, and on Monday 19 August I reported to the Cashier's Office in Pool Valley. As I remember there were about half a dozen people in the office. Conductors would pay in at one of the small windows, and one of the cashiers proper would count their cash and ensure it tallied with the waybill. The waybill and ticket machine would then be passed to the clerks, me included, for checking. As I recall (and I'm going back 50 years) the conductor would record the number from his Setright ticket machine at the beginning and end of each journey. Our job was to check the ticket numbers and the amount of cash calculated and paid in. If there was a discrepancy — 'overs' or 'shorts', as they were known — this would be deducted from or added to the conductor's wages.

I soon got to know the conductors; in the main they were a good-humoured bunch, and I loved listening to them recounting the day's events or recalling events from the past. They were a pretty motley crew, and this was reflected in their waybills. Some were good at arithmetic and some were not, some had neat handwriting and some did not — and, of course, most of the waybills would have been completed while the conductor was standing on the platform of a moving bus, so it is hardly surprising that these were frequently difficult to decipher! Once the waybill had been agreed a ticket would be run off the Setright to provide the start number for the following turn and pinned to a new waybill, which would be placed in the conductor's box.

Banking was another of the duties performed twice a day if I remember correctly. One of the cashiers, in particular, would wrap up the bank bag in newspaper and stick it in a paper bag. "Right, I've got my dripping sandwiches!" It was said in jest, but precautions did need to be taken, and, indeed, one of the cashiers was attacked on his way to the night safe while I was there. Fortunately he wasn't seriously hurt.

For me one of the perks was the position of my desk, which faced the window overlooking Pool Valley and the roofs of the buses constantly arriving and departing. The downside was that it was one of the hottest summers for a long time, and the sun beat in relentlessly. Brighton had just received its first 'Queen Marys', the VUFs, and these had been allocated to the Moulsecoomb local services that terminated in the Old Steine. How true it was I don't know, but I was told that this was because Southdown wanted a new bus station and was trying to prove to the County Borough of Brighton that 'the Valley' wasn't suitable for 30ft double-deckers. Suitable or no, it would subsequently be used not only by PD3s but, 50 years on, by 12m coaches, including six-wheel Olympians repatriated from Hong Kong, so this can scarcely be regarded as a valid argument!

Obviously the Cashier's Office was open seven days a week from early until late, (although conductors on the latest shifts would pay their takings into the night safe and have them checked the following day), so it followed that the staff were required to work shifts. On the Friday of my first week no one had mentioned a day off, so I tentatively approached the Chief Cashier. "Am I entitled to a day off this week?" "You had it," came the terse reply, "last Sunday!" I could have argued that my employment didn't start until the Monday, but, as a junior trainee of one week's standing, I decided that discretion was probably the better part of valour.

After my stint in the Cashier's Office I moved to the room next door, still part of the same section, in which various tasks were carried out. My first job in the main office was to assist the mileage clerk. Every day he would spread out a huge sheet of graph paper, on the left hand side of which (and here I'm relying on my memory again) were entered the fleet numbers of the 'cars' allocated to the Brighton area and, across the top, the services operated. The mileage operated on each route would be entered against the appropriate vehicle, and it was interesting to note from this some of the more unusual workings. Occasionally no mileage details would be received for a particular bus; this would usually turn out to be

Left: Brighton's Steine Street coach station, source of so many memories. By 24 September 1969, when this photograph was taken, the company's head office had moved to the new Southdown House, in Freshfield Road, but the coach station would remain in use for a few more years. Note the Watney's public house and the old Brighton brewer's name, 'Tamplins', which in the 1940s and '50s had adorned the sides of so many Southdown buses. *Roger Knight*

a vehicle operating on joint services 18, 119, 122 or 180, and a series of frantic phone calls would elicit the information that the vehicle in question had been borrowed by Maidstone & District and would turn up a couple of days later! Whether or not the reverse happened I never discovered.

Another of the tasks undertaken was the checking of excursion and express-coach tickets, a job I loathed. I would be handed 30 or 40 tickets — a mixture of adult/child and single/return — and asked to tot up their value. Maths had never been my strong point, and, of course, this was long before the days of calculators, so I would sit for hours, adding up the tickets over and over again, feeling more embarrassed by the minute, until I reached the same total twice and hoped it was the right one!

After three months I moved to the Wages Office — still an Area office but situated in Manchester Street, adjacent to the company's Head Office in Steine Street. We worked from 8am to 6.30pm on Monday, the busiest day, and the hours became shorter as the week went on, payday itself being on a Thursday. On Mondays someone would bring in a loaf of bread, someone else a basin of beef or pork dripping, and at about 5pm we would lay the three-bar electric fire on its back and enjoy a veritable feast of toast and dripping.

On Thursday mornings the cash for the wages would be brought from the bank, the required sums of copper, silver and notes having already been calculated. The money would then be put into brown envelopes with self-adhesive flaps and little holes so you could see what

Right: Although commonly described as being in Steine Street the coach station had its entrance in Manchester Street. This photograph, taken (like the previous shot) in the direction of St James's Street, features, on the right, the entrance to the coach station and, on the far left, the rear of the former Head Office and Brighton Area offices. As will be apparent, the location was changing rapidly, and the photographer is to be commended for recording such scenes for posterity. *Roger Knight*

was inside — remember? Each envelope bore the name of the employee together with the amount due, and these would be placed in long wooden trays, standing upright with the open flap at the top. Someone would then insert the notes, someone else the coins, and a third person would come along behind and seal the envelopes. This all had to be done by mid-day so that the wages could be delivered to the various depots and offices in time for the staff to be paid. My biggest claim to fame (or, rather, infamy) came one morning when I was given the task of sealing the wage packets. Being somewhat over-enthusiastic, I managed to seal about 250 envelopes before the money had been placed inside. I was not a popular person!

Of the various Brighton Area offices in which I worked there were two that I particularly enjoyed. One was Private Hire. Customers would contact us requesting a quotation for the hire of a coach for a particular outing over a particular route or to a specified destination. Sometimes, however, they would ask for a suggested tour. We had a handbook giving details of a number of excursions together with the mileage, from which the cost could be calculated. (I recall it had on the cover a photograph of a prewar Leyland Tiger, which I covered up with a picture of a Harrington-bodied Commer. Philistine!) Occasionally I would be asked to plan something myself, whereupon I would spend an evening with an Ordnance Survey map and one of those wheel things that measures mileage. I used to try to devise routes that were a bit different from the run-of-the-mill excursions; I never received any complaints, but I did sometimes wonder whether the roads I selected were all suitable for a 30ft x 8ft coach!

The other spell I found especially interesting was in the Coach Booking Office in Manchester Street, which gave me my first experience of dealing with the public, as well as the opportunity to listen to Beadle-Commers revving up all day! Tickets were issued from a Lamson Paragon machine that consisted of a large metal box inside which was a roll of tickets, each measuring about 4in x 3in and with two or three copies. On the top of the machine was a rectangular window through which one would write the details of the journey and fare onto the ticket. A large handle at the side was then turned and the ticket delivered — a system antiquated by today's standards, but one that worked well.

My time in the Booking Office wasn't entirely without mishap. A young couple with a baby came in late one morning, wanting to go to Bristol that evening. I looked up the times and gave them the details. "OK," said the young man, "we'll come back later and collect the tickets." They duly returned at about 6pm. "Right," I said. "Let's just check those times again." I thumbed through the ABC Coach Guide and felt a sudden surge of nausea in the pit of my stomach. "Oh" I stammered. "It only runs on Saturdays." They were perfectly polite. The young man said simply: "Thanks. We'll go by train." Oops!

The Booking Office job also involved shift work and allowed me a day off during the week, so I decided to take advantage of my 'priv' and treat my mother to a day in London. The coach provided was, to my

Left: Keeping company with a pair of Leopards – dual-purpose Northern-Counties-bodied 456 (NUF 456G) of 1969 and Weymann-bodied 147 (EUF 147D) of 1966 – in Pool Valley bus station is one of Southdown's final batch of Leyland Tiger Cub coaches, No 1145 (8145 CD) of 1962. Bodywork is Weymann's Fanfare design, as adopted by Southdown following Beadle's withdrawal from the market. The photograph was taken on 24 February 1972, by which time the livery applied to these vehicles had reverted to all-over green, relieved only by a dark-green skirt. *Roger Knight*

delight, one of the newly delivered Tiger Cubs with Weymann Fanfare bodywork, Beadle by this time having ceased production. It looked magnificent with its cream window surrounds and dark-green skirt instead of the all-over apple green previously used. Inside the brown décor had gone; the moquette was a pleasant green, with fawn leather trim, undoubtedly giving the coach a much brighter and more airy impression. Unfortunately the appearance wasn't matched by the comfort of the journey. Perhaps because this was a new coach, the brakes or clutch were particularly fierce; whatever the reason, we were thrown constantly backwards and forwards until, by the time we reached Victoria, my breakfast was threatening to make a reappearance. We returned to Brighton by train, and I later discovered that our driver had until recently been a fireman!

After six months or so I moved on to Head Office, which, although located in the same buildings as the Area Offices, was always referred to as being in Steine Street. I found the atmosphere remarkably different, much more formal and less friendly — at least, that's how it appeared to me. I certainly didn't enjoy it as much, especially when I spent every day for a month or more checking printer's proofs of timetables, one of us reading out every word and number on the timetable, the other checking it against the original submission. Regrettably at this time personal circumstances made it necessary for me to resign, and my short period of employment with Southdown Motor Services Ltd came to an end.

Although my departure from Steine Street spelled the end to any dreams I may have had of becoming MD of Southdown, it wasn't the end of my association with the company in a professional capacity. Early in 1970 I was working for British Rail in Croydon. One day on the weekly vacancy list I saw an advertisement for a job with British Transport Advertising Ltd, a subsidiary of British Rail which dealt with commercial advertising on BR property and on buses operated by most of the erstwhile BET and Tilling Group companies. In the case of the latter BTA was responsible for selling advertising space and arranging the printing of the advertisements themselves. However, due to the birth of the National Bus Company two more bus operators had been brought into the fold. One was London Country Bus Services, previously the Country Area of London Transport and whose advertising had been handled by LT, the other Southdown, which hitherto had employed a private advertising agency to deal with all aspects of the advertising carried on its buses. The vacancy was for someone to take charge of administering the advertising on behalf of these two companies – a dream job! I had always taken an interest in adverts on buses, so, ignoring the fact I would be based in Central London, I applied and was duly accepted.

My colleagues and I inherited from London Transport a set of metal filing cabinets containing trays of record cards for every LCBS vehicle, filed under the garage to which it was allocated, each showing the various advertising positions, inside and out, and the adverts currently being displayed. We instigated a similar system for Southdown: creating a record card for each bus was quite straightforward, but entering the relevant information proved more difficult; no records were available, so we had to ask the billposters, when they affixed an advertisement to a bus, to inform us of what else was on display!

London Transport staff were well trained, and dealing with them was simple — look up the record card, discover RT4515 at Dartford has a blank side and send a form to the Garage Foreman asking for a Bryant & May double-deck side to be posted; the work would usually be carried out that night, and the form returned as confirmation. Not so Southdown. The billposters had been used to having their own way and resented being told what to do. A request to affix a Caffyns lower rear to PD3 No 835 met with no response, and on querying the matter we received a terse reply: 'Couldn't find 835 — think it's gone to Portsmouth. Stuck it on 843 instead.' Trying to keep accurate records was a nightmare. Whether a certain bus carried a particular advertisement may seem immaterial, but in fact it was very important. An advertiser in Eastbourne wanted his advert displayed in the Eastbourne area, not in Chichester or Bognor Regis. There was also one nasty incident whereby we were threatened with legal action over an advertising still being displayed for a product that was no longer available, and all the stops had to be pulled out to find and cover up the offending advertisements.

Not long after I started an advertising conference was held in Brighton. BTA wanted to make its presence known so decided to advertise itself on one of the Southdown buses being used to carry delegates from the station to the Brighton Centre. Special posters in 'dayglo' orange with black lettering were printed and were to be applied to every advertising position on the selected bus, both inside and out and including a couple of positions not normally used by Southdown. In view of the importance of the project I was asked to supervise the posting. On the appointed morning I arrived at Edward Street garage to find a brand-new Northern Counties-bodied Daimler Fleetline, its green and cream paintwork gleaming. The billposters were eager to get on with their special assignment and already had one double-deck side in position, its fluorescent orange clashing with the apple green. Others followed, the other side, the staircase panel, the engine cover — it was pure sacrilege! In the end I told the chief billposter I was going for a cup of tea. "I thought you were supposed to be supervising," he said, with just a hint of sarcasm. "I'm sure you'll make a perfectly good job of it," I replied as I walked out of the garage. I just couldn't bear to watch! I went back later when it was finished, and it still made me cringe. Mind

Left: A comparison in old and new on 5 July 1971 outside the company's then head office, Southdown House, in Freshfield Road, Brighton. In the foreground is Brush-bodied petrol-engined Leyland Titan TD1 No 0813 (UF 4813) of 1929, restored by the company in the early 1960s following more than a decade in store and here displaying a 'VETERAN BUS SERVICE' board ready for the official launch of route 100 between the Palace Pier and King Alfred Leisure Centre in Hove (and soon extended to Hove Lagoon). Behind is a Northern Counties-bodied Daimler Fleetline new the previous autumn but by now plastered with bright orange advertising similar to that which so traumatised one of the authors. *Roger Knight*

you, it wasn't the first time a bus had had this effect. This was the era of the all-over advertisement; in fact Southdown had the first outside London — a 'Queen Mary' PD3 promoting Roberts' Off-Licences. It was painted in a deep orange with dark green roof and bunches of grapes and bottles all over it. Worse was to come. The second was a newly delivered flat-front Bristol VRT painted as an advert for Zetters' football pools. It resembled a psychedelic zebra, and any driver coming across it for the first time at 5.30 in the morning must have thought he'd drunk too much the night before! They weren't all ghastly, however. Rediffusion had a PD3 painted in a pleasant light blue and yellow scheme and followed this with a VR in an attractive dark blue and deep yellow. Another VR received a tan and white scheme for Old Holborn tobacco.

During the early 1960s operators all over the country bought buses with illuminated offside advertisement panels. Seemingly a good idea, they never really caught on. Southdown had two batches of Northern Counties PD3s so equipped, but with one or two exceptions they all advertised either Commercial Union insurance or 'Better Travel by Southdown', written rather unimaginatively in cream block letters on an apple-green background. The feature died a natural death, and no further buses were so fitted.

We had one billposter who was assigned to the Portsmouth area and one, with an assistant, based in Brighton but who covered the rest of the Southdown area. Disaster struck in the autumn when the Brighton man fell off a ladder and broke his leg. The work was too much for the assistant to cover on his own, so he concentrated on the west of the area while four of us from Head Office went down at weekends to deal as best we could with Brighton and Eastbourne. I was all right because I lived in Brighton, but the other three were all Londoners. One stayed with me, while the other two slept on the back seats of Burlingham Seagull-bodied Commer Avenger coaches in Moulsecoomb garage. Thus I was initiated in the art of billposting.

'Target' adverts (on the rear corner panels) were simple to fix, and lower rears, beneath the rear lower-deck windows, were reasonably straightforward, but double-deck sides were another matter. They were 17ft 6in long and came in four sections. Paper ones weren't too much of a problem, much like hanging wallpaper; as long as you pasted them well enough you could slide them into position and butt them up to the next section. Even so, you had to make sure they were in the right order, or you'd end up with something like 'Ty-Tea Phoo'! Painted advertisements meant keeping a bus off the road while it was being sign-written, so these were gradually being replaced by vinyl — a self-adhesive plastic rather like very thick Fablon, onto which the advertisement was painted or printed. Affixing a vinyl double-deck side was something else. First one had to soap the panel thoroughly to ensure the vinyl could be slid into place; failure to do this would cause the section to stick fast, and there would be little chance of moving it! Standing on a ladder, holding a 4ft length of very sticky plastic and trying not to allow two parts to touch while placing it in position on the side of a bus is not the easiest thing I've ever done.

Removing advertisements wasn't much easier. I remember one bitterly cold Sunday evening in Edward Street garage trying to prise a lower rear from the back of a Leyland Leopard. It had obviously been there for a long time and had almost welded itself to the metal. I spent about three hours with my paint scraper removing particles of vinyl about half an inch square. To make matters worse another Leopard was over the pit next to me with its engine running, discharging liberal quantities of diesel fumes into the atmosphere. The next day I was off sick!

As described earlier, tracking down a particular Southdown bus wasn't always easy. One weekend two of us set out armed with a list of buses on which we needed to post Swan Vestas advertisements ('Swanupmanship', if I remember). Over the course of the weekend we managed to find most of the buses in various depots, including Brighton's last Guy Arab, which received one, fixed with great care and tenderness! By Sunday evening we had one left to find, a 'Queen Mary' that was apparently on the 12 route from Eastbourne. We waited in Old Steine, and sure enough it arrived on time and pulled into the bus stand outside Pool Valley, where it had a short layover before proceeding to Brighton station. To the amazement of waiting passengers and passers-by we climbed precariously on to the railings and, with my colleague holding the paste bucket, I proceeded to paste the side of the bus and slide the poster into place. By the time we got to the last section the driver was getting a bit fidgety, but we did it, although I have to admit it was a but wobbly!

At this time my children were small, and, commuting to Central London every day, I hardly saw them. Eventually I cut my losses as well as my salary and took a job with Brighton Corporation's Transport Department, at a time when it was trying to convert a rear-entrance PD2 to forward-entrance for one-man operation … but that's another story.

Right: The birth of the National Bus Company coincided with the introduction of overall advertising liveries, which brought in much-needed revenue. The clean lines of the Northern Counties-bodied Leyland PD3 seemed to lend itself to such treatment, and in February 1973 No 263 (BUF 263C) was painted to the order of national TV-rental company Rediffusion, being seen thus opposite the Aquarium on Brighton seafront on 11 March. Note how the 'Southdown' badge has been retained on the front grille. *Roger Knight*

Colour television by REDIFFUSION
Rent or buy from REDIFFUSION
12
EASTBOURNE
PEACEHAVEN · NEWHAVEN
SEAFORD
BUS STOP
ARLINGTON
Wherever you live television by REDIFFUSION
REDIFFUSION
Colour TV by
Southdown
263
REDIFFUSION
BUF 263C

7. THE WINDS OF CHANGE

Between my spells of working for and with Southdown a great many changes had taken place. In 1961 the Brighton Area Transport Services (BATS) agreement had come into force, all services within the designated area being co-ordinated, and revenue and mileage pooled on a percentage basis. Southdown's protective fares were swept away, bus stops became common to all three operators, and Southdown buses began to be seen in some unfamiliar places. On occasions they were even seen operating former Brighton trolleybus routes! One of the most memorable sights was of red-and-cream BH&D Bristols entering the hallowed ground of Pool Valley. Initially while operating over former Southdown routes they carried green slip-boards proclaiming 'On hire to Southdown Motor Services'.

There were still a few prewar Leylands running around, but these were fast disappearing. Inroads were also being made into the utility

Above: Many enthusiasts, the authors included, collected timetables, and Southdown's was a prized possession. Simple and to the point, its cover featured an approximation of a Park Royal-bodied Leyland PD1 on the 12 – a route on which such a bus would likely have struggled.
John Bishop collection

Right: Having arrived from Brighton, all-Leyland PD1 No 300 (HCD 900) of 1947 pauses on Worthing seafront before resuming its journey to Arundel on route 10. Behind is No 341 (JCD 41), one of the 1948 batch of all-Leyland PD2s, many of which were used on Worthing town services.
A. D. Packer

Guys, although many of these had been subject to smart open-top conversion at Portslade Works and were maintaining the open-top services at Brighton, Worthing and Hayling Island.

During this time my work took me regularly to Worthing, where the town services were operated mainly by the remaining closed-top utility Guys, including some that had received 'new' East Lancs bodies removed from withdrawn Leyland TD2s that were rarely seen in Brighton. The Guys were replaced in Worthing by the JCD-registered all-Leyland PD2/1s, which in turn gave way to Park Royal-bodied Guy Arab IVs cascaded from country services when these were taken over by one-man operated single-deckers.

I frequently travelled on the 9 and 10, which reached Worthing via the old wooden toll bridge at Shoreham and North Lancing before carrying on to Littlehampton and Arundel respectively. These two routes were operated regularly by the Leyland PD1s with Leyland or Park Royal bodywork. I can still hear their ponderous tickover, so slow that it seemed they must inevitably stall. With their small-capacity engines they had been no match for the PD2s on front-line services but were quite happy pottering along the flat West Sussex coastal strip. I remember returning from Eastbourne one hot summer's day when an all-Leyland PD1 was pressed into service as relief to the usual PD2/12. Both buses left Eastbourne with full loads, but halfway up Sanatorium Hill the PD1 spluttered to a halt, and half the passengers were asked to get off and walk! Ironically a Park Royal-bodied PD1 climbing this very hill was depicted on the front of the Southdown timetable for many years.

As far as double-deckers were concerned, throughout the 1960s the PD3 reigned supreme, although subtle changes to the design meant that buses of the final batch would look quite different from those received in 1958. The earliest deliveries had the

Left Southdown's first Northern Counties-bodied Leyland Titan PD3s arrived in 1958, and deliveries continued for almost a decade. This photograph of No 899 (2899 CD), gleaming and unsullied by advertisements, was taken in Brighton's Pool Valley bus station when the bus was new in the spring 1961. Note the comprehensive destination display. *John Bishop / Online Transport Archive*

Left: Delivered in 1961/2, the 40 Leyland PD3/5 models fitted with semi-automatic transmission struggled on Southdown's hilly routes in the Brighton and Eastbourne areas and as a result tended to be confined to the flatter terrain of Portsmouth and the West Sussex coastal strip. In this view No 940 (6940 CD) pauses on Worthing seafront between journeys to and from Lancing on local service 7. The offside of these vehicles featured an illuminated advertisement panel, here being used to promote Harrington Motors, the same company that bodied so many Southdown vehicles. *Gerald Mead*

characteristic Northern Counties front windows with heavily radiused top corners, and they quickly became dated, if also rather quaint. The 1958 batch had the traditional Southdown brown interior, but this was replaced on the following year's deliveries by a rather uninspiring dark green moquette. Later batches had an attractive light green, dark green and beige moquette, with seat backs and side panels in dark wood-grain Formica, giving them the high-class look one had come to expect from Southdown. Throughout, the company continued to specify its own design of seat, with back somewhat higher than normal and shaped to fit the contours of the occupant. The only significant mechanical variation came in 1961/2 in the form of a batch of 40 PD3/5s, with pneumocyclic transmission, many of which ended up on Worthing town services due to their poor hill-climbing abilities. Then, of course, there were the 30 convertible open-toppers of 1964/5, which replaced the utility Guys. The final incarnation was the 'panoramic', with, on the upper deck, just three main side windows and wrap-around front windows. In my opinion the design failed miserably, the bus being too short to suit the extra-long windows, while the rearmost side window on the lower deck, with downswept upper edge, looked incongruous and anachronistic.

As had so often been the case Southdown clung to tradition, the front-engined double-decker remaining the choice for as long as was possible, and it was not until 1970 that the first rear-engined 'deckers entered the main Southdown fleet. In view of its long association with Leyland it might have been expected that Southdown would opt for the Atlantean, but instead it chose the Daimler Fleetline, with Gardner engine. The bodywork was less of a surprise, being by Northern Counties and very much a development of that fitted to the 'panoramic' PD3s but much more pleasing to the eye. Internally these buses were to the usual specification, and, unlike some operators, which were cramming 78 passengers into a rear-engined 'decker, Southdown specified a mere 71, these being still of the contoured type; in fact there was almost room to hold a dance at the front of the upper deck! By this time Southdown was part of the National Bus Company, and the Fleetlines were actually preceded into service by the first standard-issue Bristol VRTs, these having been diverted from BH&D, under Southdown control since the start of the NBC era. Unfortunately the Fleetlines were found to have excessively heavy steering, and following trade-union complaints most were transferred to that home for unloved buses, Worthing! Nevertheless, they were the last true Southdown double-deckers; a second batch, with Leyland engines, arrived in 1972, but these had ECW bodywork. By this time the standard double-decker was the ECW-bodied Bristol VRT, although the company would finally receive some Atlanteans – with handsome Park Royal bodywork, finished by Roe – in two batches in 1974/5.

The other major development during the 1960s was the expansion of one-man operation (OMO). The increase in the permitted length of single-deckers to 36ft meant that a saloon could carry almost as many passengers as a conventional 27ft 6in double-decker and without

Right: In the late 1950s, to facilitate one-man operation, the East Lancs-bodied Leyland Royal Tiger buses were rebuilt with front entrances. One of the first batch, No 1505 (LUF 505) of 1952 gives little clue as to its former rear-entrance layout in this view at Emsworth garage. *John Bishop / Online Transport Archive*

Left: The last Leyland Tiger Cub service buses, bodied by Marshall of Cambridge, arrived in 1962, among them 662 (7662 CD), seen in West Worthing on 3 May 1964. *Gerald Mead*

the need for a conductor. With falling passenger numbers and increasing wages and fuel costs it was hardly surprising that OMO was seen as a means of salvation, even though in the event the passengers put off by longer journey times probably offset the financial gain.

By this time the Royal Tigers had all been converted to front-entrance, and a handful of Tiger Cubs bought to the same configuration, but it was in 1963 that the single-deck revolution really began. The standard vehicle was the 36ft Leyland Leopard with bodywork to the standard BET design by Marshall, Weymann or Willowbrook. The early deliveries had seating for 51, average for the time, but, in the face of trade-union objections, Southdown reduced them to 45-seaters, and all later batches were of this capacity. Gradually all but the busiest of services were converted to single-deck OMO, a great pity from the passenger's point of view – quite literally, for no longer was the old adage 'you see more from the top of a bus' applicable.

The Leopards were joined in 1968 by the company's first Bristol REs, the manufacturer now being allowed to sell on the open market. It seemed strange that with the amalgamation yet to come, both Southdown and BH&D were taking into stock the same type of vehicle, something that would have been unheard of a few years earlier. The first REs for Southdown were 36ft long and with Gardner engines, but in 1970 came a batch of 33ft RESLs with Leyland 680 engines, making them extremely fast and manœuvrable. They were put to work on Brighton service 38, which had in its time been worked by all three Brighton operators. The route ran from the Bevendean Hospital, close to the Race Course, descended to Lewes Road and crossed town to Seven Dials, Clock Tower, West Street and (since the BATS agreement) Pool Valley. It was a particularly hilly route and for most of its length ran through heavy traffic, a round trip involving something like 70 gear changes. Add to this its tight timings, and it is easy to understand why it became known as the 'race track'.

When I first moved to the Lewes Road area the 38 was worked by Brighton Corporation AEC Regents with preselector gearboxes, which were probably ideally suited to the terrain. In the early 1950s the service passed to BH&D, which used brand-new Bristol KSWs, these being replaced in 1959 by the company's first Bristol Lodekkas, both types handling the route capably. The same could not be said of the PD2/12s and Guy Arabs that took over after the route passed to Southdown, and the East Lancs-bodied PD2s proved particularly troublesome: when they were parked on one of Brighton's steepest hills their sliding doors would shudder and groan into action – or, as often, not, refusing to open at all until the bus was on more level ground. The RESLs must have come as quite a relief to drivers and passengers alike. Again, these were the last true Southdown single-deckers. Three more RELLs followed with standard ECW bodies, and then came Leyland Nationals.

INTERNATIONAAL
THEATERFESTIVAL
3 APRIL - 22 MEI 1962
HOLLAND
8737 CD
3 MERKSEM
CHOCOLADE
COTE D'OR
SUIKERWAREN
PORTO
SHERRY

For its coaching requirements Southdown flirted briefly with Weymann before settling on tried and tested local supplier Thomas Harrington. The latter had recently introduced its classic Cavalier design, and those supplied on Leyland Leopard chassis were arguably the most attractive and stylish coaches ever owned by Southdown. Unfortunately Harrington followed in the footsteps of Beadle and ceased production. It then became a choice of Duple or Plaxton … or nothing. The same high standard of interior was maintained, but externally their products lacked the character and individuality of previous coaches.

And then the inevitable happened: the National Bus Company imposed its corporate identity and drab, uninspiring liveries. Although vehicles continued to display the proud fleetname on their sides, the true character of Southdown was smothered.

Right: Having largely ignored its local coachbuilder since the war, Southdown returned to Thomas Harrington of Hove in 1961, taking 30 examples of the Cavalier design on Leyland's then new Leopard L2T coach chassis. The combination of the body's handsome lines and Southdown's new touring-coach livery, with cream upper half, made these extremely attractive vehicles and set a standard for other operators to match. An immaculate 1718 (2718 CD) makes the point in Huddersfield during its first summer of service. *John Bishop / Online Transport Archive*

Left: Further Leopard/ Harrington Cavalier touring coaches arrived in readiness for the following season, and this splendid picture features car 1737 (8737 CD) rubbing shoulders with PCC trams in Antwerp in April 1962. When new these vehicles were fitted with just 28 seats, in 2+1 formation, thereby maintaining the Southdown tradition of putting passenger comfort before capacity. *Bruce Jenkins*

Right: Exeter coach station is the location for this fine offside view of No 1753 (753 DCD), numerically the last of 54 Harrington Cavalier-bodied Leyland Leopards delivered in the period 1961-3, although the final five, including 1753, were effectively prototypes for the later Grenadier design. *Gerald Mead*

102
409
DCD
409
31
954
CUF
954

Far left: Marine Parade, Brighton, just outside the town's Pool Valley bus station and opposite the Palace Pier, is the setting for this unusual view of two Northern Counties-bodied Leyland PD3 'Queen Marys' delivered in 1964. Convertible No 409 (409 DCD), in open-top form, is loaded with passengers on service 102 between Arundel and Devil's Dyke, while 954 (954 CUF) has just arrived at the end of its long journey from Portsmouth on the 31. Happily both vehicles survive, 409 retained by the company as a 'heritage' vehicle and 954 in private ownership, having recently been restored. *Roger Knight*

Left: The 285 Leyland PD3s purchased by Southdown in the period 1958-67 included a few oddities. Delivered in 1965, No 257 (BUF 257C) was fitted with an experimental system of heating and ventilation. Distinguishable by its curved lower-deck windscreen and offside grille, it is seen departing Pool Valley for Worthing and Littlehampton in February 1967. *Bruce Jenkins*

Left: The final PD3s were the 'Panoramics', the nickname deriving from the elongated side windows with which they were fitted. First to arrive, following exhibition at the 1966 Commercial Motor Show, was No 315 (GUF 250D), which continued the heating/ventilation experiments pioneered on No 257 and, uniquely, had curved windscreens on both decks. Seen parked in Brighton's Old Steine in February 1967 at the end of its journey from Eastbourne, it would be joined later that year by the remainder of the batch. *Bruce Jenkins*

Right: Rugged vehicles, the Park Royal-bodied Guy Arabs of 1955/6 served Southdown well, a number surviving into the early 1970s. Looking rather sorry for itself, No 550 (PUF 650), from the second batch, rests in Brighton's Old Steine on 4 March 1970 between journeys on local service 15. *Roger Knight*

Right: Nearing the end of its Southdown career, Guy Arab/Park Royal No 553 (PUF 653) rests inside Brighton's Freshfield Road garage, normally used only by coaches. Interestingly the rear number screen shows '42', this being a former trolleybus route normally operated by Brighton Corporation but on which, under the terms of the BATS agreement, Southdown would work the occasional journey to balance mileage.
Roger Knight

Top left: Near-contemporaries of the Guy Arabs, the final PD2/12s, delivered 1956/7, also survived until the 1970s. With destination screen masked to display a single line but otherwise in fine condition, Beadle-bodied 782 (RUF 182) is seen parked between a pair of PD3s – one of them a recently delivered 'Panoramic' – inside Worthing depot. Beautifully restored, No 786 from the same batch represents this type among the ranks of preserved Southdown vehicles. *Roger Knight*

Top rightt: Southdown's last half-cabs in normal service were withdrawn in 1971, and in anticipation of this the Southdown Enthusiasts' Club organised a commemorative tour. Still in pristine condition, East Lancs-bodied Leyland PD2/12 No 807 (RUF 207) poses on the forecourt of Chichester garage on 31 July. *Roger Knight*

Left: East Lancs-bodied PD2/12 No 800 (RUF 200) shows off its handsome lines outside Portsmouth's Hyde Park Road garage on 31 August 1971. The condition of this vehicle, even down to the retention of a full destination display, is especially noteworthy, and it is difficult to believe that within a month it would be on its way to Frank Cowley, a Salford-based dealer who at this time purchased the majority of Southdown's redundant stock. Happily similar No 805 survives in preservation to remind us of past glories. *Roger Knight*

Right: Anathema to traditionalists who believe a bus should have its engine at the front and, ideally, an open platform at the rear, the Northern Counties-bodied Daimler Fleetlines delivered in the autumn of 1970 were nevertheless fine vehicles that were more than worthy of carrying the Southdown name. Delivered in traditional livery, complete with shaded block fleetname and scroll badge on the front, a number were used initially on local services in the Brighton area. Still looking new, 381 (TCD 381J) was photographed in Lower Bevendean on 29 April 1971.
Roger Knight

Right: Still in service as the 1970s dawned were all but one of the 285 Northern Counties-bodied Leyland PD3s delivered in the years 1958-67. In this view, recorded in April 1971, a 10-year-old No 904 (2904 CD) emerges from Sussex University onto the A27 Brighton–Lewes road – a manœuvre impossible following reconstruction of this road as a dual-carriageway.
Roger Knight

Left: The spread of one-man operation rendered the crew-operated PD3s redundant throughout much of Southdown's traditional operating territory, and many saw out their days on the busy Brighton area routes inherited from BH&D, which would be among the last converted to OMO. One of the earlier examples of its type, delivered in 1959, No 830 (VUF 830) nevertheless looked like new when photographed on 26 July 1971 at Rottingdean. The 2 was one of the ex-BH&D routes, but by this time the decision had been to phase out the traditional BH&D livery of red and cream, and the only distinction from Southdown 'proper' lay in the fleetname, which upon close scrutiny can be seen to read 'SOUTHDOWN-BH&D'. *Roger Knight*

Left: As part of an experiment to make its large fleet of PD3s suitable for one-man operation No 961 (961 CUF) of 1963 was equipped with a driver's ticket machine mounted on the front bulkhead, while at the rear it was fitted with a reversing window (in the emergency door) and reversing lights. Ultimately it was decided not to pursue the experiment, but No 961 nevertheless looked very smart when photographed on 3 September 1971 in Boundary Road, Hove, on service 6 – ironically one of the crew routes inherited from BH&D! *Roger Knight*

Right: NBC influence started to make itself felt in 1970 with the delivery of 10 ECW-bodied Bristol VRTs intended originally for BH&D, which Southdown had absorbed the previous year. When photographed in Lewes bus station on 29 April 1971 No 504 (SCD 504H) was – notwithstanding the confused destination display – bound for Tunbridge Wells. *Roger Knight*

Bottom: Although both London Country and Southdown were by now under NBC control there was, to the casual observer, little evidence of this on 10 March 1972 at Tunbridge Wells coach station, where Green Line route 704 from Windsor met with Southdown's 119 from Brighton. Heresy though it might be for some, Bristol VRT/ECW No 506 (TCD 506J) looks quite cheerful compared with Routemaster 'coach' RCL2256. Tunbridge Wells was in fact Maidstone & District territory, although Southdown buses would penetrate as far as Gravesend on route 122, worked jointly with M&D. *Roger Knight*

Far right: Things did not always run smoothly. Seen outside St Peter's Church, in London Road, Brighton, on a murky 31 January 1972, an unidentified Bristol VRT from the 1970 batch receives assistance from ex-BH&D Bristol K5G No W4 (EAP 4), cut down as a towing vehicle and by now in Southdown green with 'SOUTHDOWN-BH&D' fleetnames. *Roger Knight*

13
111 AP

Right: In the 1960s Southdown took delivery of numerous Leyland Leopards with bus bodywork to standard BET Federation design and built variously by Marshall, Weymann and Willowbrook. At first glance a standard Leopard/Willowbrook, No 480 (EUF 224D) had been new in 1966 as a Plaxton-bodied coach (numbered 1224) but was rebodied as a bus following major accident damage sustained two years later. It is pictured in Brighton's Old Steine on 29 April 1971, at which time BH&D buses, such as the Bristol FLF Lodekka on the left, were still red but those of the Corporation, represented by the newly delivered Leyland Atlantean, were starting to turn blue. *Roger Knight*

Bottom: Although Southdown had favoured the rear-engined Bristol RE – with BET-style Marshall bodywork – from 1968, a further sign of NBC influence was the delivery in March 1971 of three ECW-bodied examples. Although representing a change of policy these perfectly proportioned vehicles nevertheless looked superb in the company's traditional livery, as demonstrated by No 601 (UCD 601J) in Beaconsfield Villas, Brighton, near the end of its journey from Haywards Heath on 2 May 1971. *Roger Knight*

Far right: Unusual vehicles delivered in the latter half of 1969 were a batch of 30 Leyland Leopards with dual-purpose Northern Counties bodywork. The intention was that they should work as buses in the off-season and duplicate express coaches in the summer months, but when photographed on a gloriously sunny 17 July 1971 No 465 (PUF 165H) was parked on Brighton's Madeira Drive ready for excursion duty. Following the introduction of NBC's corporate image these vehicles would adopt green and white 'local coach' livery, in which garb this example is now preserved. *Roger*

EXCURSION 000
GLENSIDE HO
Southdown
Southdown
PLEASE PAY AS YOU ENTER
465
PUF 165H

Right: By the early 1960s Southdown's traditional suppliers of coach bodywork were diminishing in number, and in 1964 the company took delivery of its first six examples of Plaxton's Panorama body, on Leyland Leopard chassis. A further 10 of this combination arrived in 1965, including No 1188 (BUF 88C), photographed on 2 September 1973 at Battersea coach park, where express coaches would park up during the day before returning home in the evening. *Gerald Mead*

Bottom: It was a sad day when Southdown's traditional green gave way to the bland National white, as seen on Leopard/ Plaxton 1204 (EUF 204D) at Battersea on 12 August 1973, although the retention of chrome hub caps helped maintain that extra touch of class always associated with the company. *Gerald Mead*

Far right: The last Southdown vehicles bodied by Harrington, to the Hove builder's new Grenadier style, were a batch of 10 Leyland Leopards delivered in 1965. Thus far defying the march of National white, No 1763 (BUF 163C) – the very last – is pictured on a visit to Aylesford Priory, near Maidstone, in September 1974. *Bruce*

PRIVATE
Southdown
BUF 163C

LINCOLNSHIRE
HCD 386E
Southdown

Far left: Following the demise as a coachbuilder of Thomas Harrington Southdown turned for its touring coaches to Duple. One of a batch of 25 Duple Commander-bodied Leyland Leopards delivered in 1967 was 1786 (HCD 386E), pictured while on tour on 8 May 1971. *Roger Knight*

Left: Southdown's last 'proper' touring coaches, delivered in the company's traditional livery and fitted with 2+1 seating, were a batch of Plaxton Panorama Elite-bodied Leopards received in 1971. Numerically the last of all (albeit not the last to arrive) was No 1844 (UUF 344J), photographed on 25 September 1971 outside Brighton's Royal Pavilion; what better setting for a Southdown coach? Later in their lives a number of this batch would revert to traditional green, initially to mark the company's 65th anniversary. *Roger Knight*

Right: The later 'Queen Mary' PD3s survived long enough to be repainted in NBC leaf-green livery, among them No 289 (FCD 289D) of 1966, seen in Worthing on 16 August 1973. Note, however, that the driver (right) still wears traditional Southdown summer uniform. *Gerald Mead*

Right: Pending repaint in leaf green vehicles still in traditional colours had their gold-leaf fleetnames replaced by NBC's corporate style. Demonstrating the effect in Lewes Road, Brighton, on 16 August 1973 is No 355 (HCD 355E), one of the final, 1967 batch of PD3/4s, with Northern Counties bodywork of updated appearance and incorporating panoramic windows. *Gerald Mead*

Left: NBC's standard double-decker for most of its existence was the Bristol VRT with ECW bodywork, and among those operated by Southdown were eight acquired in 1973 from Scottish Omnibuses in exchange for ex-BH&D FLF Lodekkas. Identifiable by its distinctive SBG-style destination screen and its extra length (33ft instead of 30ft), No 543 (LFS 289F) emerges from Brighton station in September 1978. Note that by now route 110 served Newhaven rather than Bevendean!
Bruce Jenkins

Left: In the late 1970s there was little to relieve the unremitting diet of leaf green. Approaching Brighton's Old Steine (and obscuring the narrow western exit from Edward Street garage), ECW-bodied Bristol VRT No 525 (WCD 525K) of 1971 shows off the gold band applied to celebrate the golden anniversary of Southdown's central works in Victoria Road, Portslade, although the cryptic legend scarcely does justice to all the skilful work carried out over the years by the staff there. This view was recorded in September 1978.
Bruce Jenkins

8. KEEPING THE MEMORIES ALIVE

'Not dead but sleeping' is a description that might well have been applied to Southdown during its days under NBC control, and it seemed that every opportunity was taken to revive the traditional livery and fleetname. In 1980, to mark the company's 65th anniversary, a couple of Plaxton-bodied Leyland Leopard coaches were treated to a repaint in full apple-green livery, complete with scroll fleetnames, while two double-deckers escaped NBC leaf green, surviving throughout in traditional green and cream. Ironically both were ex-BH&D Bristol Lodekkas, and in 1986 they passed to the reactivated BH&D company, which restored them to their original livery cream and black. Even a pair of Ford Transit minibuses used on the Cuckmere Community Bus operation received apple green and cream, complete with dark-green lining.

Privatisation of the company in 1987 was like emerging into the light at the end of the tunnel. Ahead of privatisation many companies had adopted the colours they had worn in pre-NBC days but in new applications, but Southdown reverted to its traditional livery (albeit with slightly less cream on double-deckers), making even Leyland Nationals look presentable!

Further evidence of a return to pre-NBC standards was apparent in 1989 with the arrival of 12 (yes, we were back to ordering in dozens!) Volvo B10M Citybuses with Northern Counties bodywork fitted with semi-coach seats. Alas the renaissance proved short-lived, and later that year the company was sold to Stagecoach Holdings, and green and cream gave way to Stagecoach stripes. Worse was to come: in 1992 the company was divided, and Sussex Coastline Buses, as Southdown Motor Services had been renamed, confined itself to activities in West Sussex and Hampshire. 'Southdown' clung on for a while as a fleetname (ironically on buses in *East* Sussex), but in 1993 that too disappeared.

It seemed that Southdown was finally dead. Yet still it refused to lie down. In 2002 the management of Sussex Coastline Buses, mindful of the historic significance of their company's former title – and its value

Right: With the impending break-up of the National Bus Company and deregulation just around the corner came a return of Southdown's much-loved apple green and cream livery. For a while it seemed as though the good old days had returned, and the rain does nothing to spoil this September 1986 view of Eastern Coach Works-bodied Bristol VRT 553 (NCD 553M), complete with dark-green wheels, in Seaside, Eastbourne.
Bruce Jenkins

Left: The Stagecoach takeover in 1989 brought to an end the green-and-cream-revival, the Perth-based group imposing its corporate livery of white with multi-coloured stripes, but in 1990 a Bristol VRT was repainted in *full* traditional livery, complete with dark-green lining, to mark Southdown's 75th anniversary. No 276 (JWV 976W) seen thus adorned inside Worthing garage. *John Bishop / Online Transport Archive*

Left: The only new vehicles purchased by Southdown during the brief period of independence between NBC and Stagecoach ownership were 12 Northern Counties-bodied Volvo B10M double-deckers, among them 305 (F305 MYJ), pictured *c*1990 alongside the traditional 'SOUTHDOWN' sign at the exit of Worthing garage. Delivered in 1989, they would give yeoman service, the last being retired as recently as 2008. *John Bishop / Online Transport Archive*

Right: What might have been, had not Southdown been bought out by Stagecoach in 1989. Wearing full Southdown-style apple-green and cream livery, Northern Counties-bodied Leyland Olympian G541 VBB, new to Kentish Bus but by now with Renown Travel, heads into Eastbourne along King's Drive near the District General Hospital on 7 February 2007. *Glyn Kraemer-Johnson*

to potential competitors – decided to resurrect it, with the result that Southdown Motor Services Ltd is once again the major provider of bus services in West Sussex and east Hampshire. Moreover, the affection and respect in which 'Southdown' is held is borne out by the number of other operators that have adopted its traditional colours. One of the first was Emsworth & District, followed shortly by Village Bus, of Findon, and when the late David Howard established his Eastbourne-based 'Cavendish Motor Services' it was with a stroke of genius that he adopted the full Southdown livery for its vehicles. Any number of passengers were heard to remark how nice it was to have 'the old green-and-cream buses' back, but history has since repeated itself, Stagecoach taking over both the Cavendish operation and municipally owned Eastbourne Buses, with which it was set up to compete.

A vast number of former Southdown buses survive in preservation, the total being bettered perhaps only by those of London Transport. The Amberley Working Museum, near Arundel, is dedicated to preserving the area's rural and industrial heritage and includes on site a country bus garage typical of those once to be found throughout Sussex. Its collection of Southdown vehicles includes a pair of Tilling-Stevens saloons, a Dennis 30cwt, a Leyland N and a number of TD1 double-deckers. Elsewhere, more modern vehicles preserved include Bristol VRTs and Leyland Nationals and, from the intervening half-century, Leyland TDs, PS1s and PD2s plus, of course, numerous examples of the 'Queen Mary' PD3 – a type that seems to be second in popularity only to the Routemaster. Also represented are the Leyland Cub, Tiger Cub and Guy Arab IV, while currently undergoing restoration is an open-top utility Guy Arab that has been repatriated from the Netherlands. It is thanks to the hard work and enthusiasm of these preservationists that it is still possible, at events such as the annual Worthing Running Day, to ride on traditional Southdown vehicles and relive memories of a company that was most definitely a cut above the rest.

Left: Leyland N No 125 (CD 5125), new in 1920 as a Harrington bodied saloon but now with a Short Bros double-deck body, is today resident at the Amberley Working Museum, where, thanks to a dedicated team of enthusiasts, it enables visitors to relive their Southdown memories. It is pictured at the annual gathering in September 1985 alongside Brighton, Hove & District Bristol Lodekka RPN 10, at that time still in service with Southdown and destined to see further use with the newly reactivated BH&D company. *Online Transport Archive*

Left: The open-top Brush-bodied Leyland Titan TD1s of 1929 survived into the postwar years, when they could be seen plying between Brighton and Devil's Dyke. One of the last survivors was No 813 (UF 4813), which became part of the service fleet and could often be found at Southdown's central works in Victoria Road, Portslade. Many photographs show the front, but not many the rear, with sweeping outside staircase; this view features the bus at an early London–Brighton Historic Vehicle Commercial Club rally in the early 1960s after its first restoration by Southdown Motor Services but before the application of period advertisements. *John Bishop / Online Transport Archive*

Above: By the 1930s, after a period standardising on Tilling-Stevens chassis, Southdown had switched allegiance to Leyland Motors. No 928 (UF 7428), one of the Short-bodied batch of Titan TD1s with petrol engines, was a pioneer in the world of bus preservation, having been acquired for this purpose in 1959. It eventually joined the collection at Amberley Working Museum, where it was fully restored, and is seen here participating in one of the Broad Street Depot Museum's running days in Old Portsmouth. Sadly the depot, which housed many vehicles and became something of a tourist attraction in its own right, has since been vacated to make way for the redevelopment of the area. *John Bishop / Online Transport Archive*

Above: A remarkable survivor from the 1920s is this charming Short-bodied Dennis 30cwt saloon, No 517 (UF 1517), of 1927. The bus ran in service for just six years before being sold for use as a summer house but thanks to its all-metal construction survived for long enough to be purchased for preservation by Amberley Working Museum. This vehicle is seen on the occasion the popular annual Worthing Running Day in 2006, in which year the majority of vehicles were on display along the coast at Shoreham-by-Sea. *John Bishop / Online Transport Archive*

Left: The body of No 517 pictured *c*1957 in the garden of a house in the village of Fulking, not far from Devil's Dyke. *John Bishop / Online Transport Archive*

Above: In the eyes of many the perfect single-deck body was the functional postwar Eastern Coach Works design as fitted to Leyland Tiger PS1 No 677 (GUF 727). Delivered in 1947 as a coach, numbered 1227, this vehicle was rebuilt in 1955 as a bus and, with the full screen and dark-green roof, arguably looked even better than it had when new. Nowadays preserved in Lincolnshire, it made a welcome return to Sussex in 2005 for a retiring Southdown employee at Worthing and also attended that year's Magnificent Motors rally in Eastbourne, where it stirred many happy memories, not least among the authors! *John Bishop / Online Transport Archive*